P9-CCH-396

Stunning Stitches

stunning
STITCHES

21 SHAWLS, SCARVES, AND COWLS
YOU'LL LOVE TO KNIT

Jen Lucas

Martingale®
Create with Confidence

Stunning Stitches:
21 Shawls, Scarves, and Cowls You'll Love to Knit
© 2017 by Jen Lucas

Martingale®
19021 120th Ave. NE, Ste. 102
Bothell, WA 98011-9511 USA
ShopMartingale.com

No part of this product may be reproduced in any form, unless otherwise stated, in which case reproduction is limited to the use of the purchaser. The written instructions, photographs, designs, projects, and patterns are intended for the personal, noncommercial use of the retail purchaser and are under federal copyright laws; they are not to be reproduced by any electronic, mechanical, or other means, including informational storage or retrieval systems, for commercial use. Permission is granted to photocopy patterns for the personal use of the retail purchaser. Attention teachers: Martingale encourages you to use this book for teaching, subject to the restrictions stated above.

The information in this book is presented in good faith, but no warranty is given nor results guaranteed. Since Martingale has no control over choice of materials or procedures, the company assumes no responsibility for the use of this information.

Printed in China
22 21 20 19 18 17   8 7 6 5 4 3 2 1

Library of Congress Cataloging-in-Publication Data
is available upon request.

ISBN: 978-1-60468-823-8

MISSION STATEMENT

We empower makers who use fabric and yarn
to make life more enjoyable.

CREDITS

PUBLISHER AND
CHIEF VISIONARY OFFICER
Jennifer Erbe Keltner

CONTENT DIRECTOR
Karen Costello Soltys

MANAGING EDITOR
Tina Cook

ACQUISITIONS EDITOR
Karen M. Burns

TECHNICAL EDITOR
Beth Bradley

COPY EDITOR
Durby Peterson

PRODUCTION MANAGER
Regina Girard

COVER AND
INTERIOR DESIGNER
Adrienne Smitke

PHOTOGRAPHER
Brent Kane

ILLUSTRATOR
Sandy Huffaker

CONTENTS

Introduction

As a designer, I'm constantly inspired by the stitch patterns that fill the stitch dictionaries on my bookshelves. The patterns are so beautiful, interesting, and thought-provoking. I can spend hours poring over them, searching for just the right pattern for my design. The hardest (and perhaps saddest) part of designing is that many times I use a stitch pattern only once. I'll add a beautiful cable and lace panel to a shawl and then mark in my stitch dictionary that I used it. It feels like it's gone forever.

In this book, I'm trying something new: accessories to be worn around your neck that use the same stitch pattern more than once. It's been a fun challenge coming up with many different items to wear as neck accessories. You'll find seven different sets, each containing three designs that feature the same stitch pattern. Sometimes you'll find a lace pattern covering an entire shawl, as in the Bampton Shawl (page 55), and then you'll see it featured at the edge of a cowlette (page 51).

Some stitch patterns are too beautiful to use just once. My hope is that you'll find yourself in love with these patterns and want to make all three accessories in the set!

~ *Jen*

CYPRUS TRIO

Simple knits and purls—that's all it takes to make this beautiful stitch pattern. Whether you're an adventurous beginner or an advanced knitter looking for a relaxing project, you're sure to enjoy creating these richly textured pieces. Choose from dickey, cowl, and stole patterns, grab a soft and squishy yarn, and you're ready for some happy knitting.

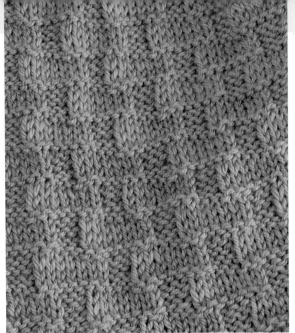

Cyprus Dickey

DESIGNED AND KNIT BY THE AUTHOR

I often wear a scarf tucked into my coat in the winter, but it can be a bit bulky and cumbersome. I loved the idea of a dickey-style scarf that provides warmth without all the bulk, so I designed this one! Worked flat, the pattern calls for intentionally twisting the fabric before joining the two ends with Kitchener stitch. When you wear it, it looks as though you have a much longer scarf stuffed into your coat or jacket—it's magic!

 Featured Yarn
1 skein of Shepherd Sport from Lorna's Laces (100% superwash merino wool; 2 oz; 200 yds) in color Growth

SKILL LEVEL: Intermediate

FINISHED CIRCUMFERENCE: 40", slightly stretched

FINISHED WIDTH: 6"

MATERIALS

185 yards of sport weight yarn (2)

US size 5 (3.75 mm) knitting needles, or size required for gauge

Size G (6.0 mm) crochet hook
Waste yarn
Tapestry needle
Blocking supplies

GAUGE

24 sts and 28 rows = 4" in patt

Gauge is not critical in this patt, but a different gauge will affect yardage and size of dickey.

PATTERN NOTES

Chart is on page 11. If you prefer to follow written instructions for the charted material, see "Written Instructions for Chart" on page 11.

While the right side and wrong side of the piece do look different, they're both textured. You may find it helpful to add a stitch marker to the right side of the work so you don't lose your place.

Stunning Stitches

» Working the Kitchener stitch with the right side and wrong side together makes the scarf into a Mobius loop.

INSTRUCTIONS

For a provisional cast on, use waste yarn and a crochet hook to chain a minimum of 37 sts.

Set-up row (RS): with knitting needle and yarn for project, PU 37 sts through the back bump of each ch, turn work.

Knit 3 rows.

Work dickey chart 28 times (224 rows). Work rows 1–3 of dickey chart once more.

Knit 3 rows.

FINISHING

Carefully undo crochet ch from provisional CO and place live sts (37 sts) onto knitting needle. Fold fabric in half and create twist, so that both ends have RS facing in same direction. Use Kitchener st to graft together (see page 93).

Block dickey to finished measurements given at beg of patt. With tapestry needle, weave in ends.

WRITTEN INSTRUCTIONS FOR CHART

If you prefer to follow row-by-row written instructions rather than a chart, use the instructions below.

Row 1 (RS): K2, P3, *K7, P3; rep from * to last 2 sts, K2.

Row 2 (WS): K2, *K3, P7; rep from * to last 5 sts, K5.

Row 3: Rep row 1.

Row 4: Knit all sts.

Row 5: K5, *K2, P3, K5; rep from * to last 2 sts, K2.

Row 6: K2, *P5, K3, P2; rep from * to last 5 sts, P3, K2.

Row 7: Rep row 5.

Row 8: Knit all sts.

Rep rows 1–8 for patt.

Cyprus Dickey Chart

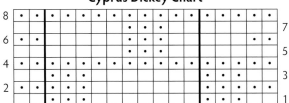

Repeat = 10 sts

Chart Legend

☐ K on RS, P on WS

⊡ P on RS, K on WS

Stunning Stitches

Cyprus Cowl

DESIGNED BY THE AUTHOR AND KNIT BY MELISSA RUSK

With knits and purls creating the texture for this cowl, it looks great whether the right side or wrong side is showing. A bulky-weight yarn makes the cowl extra comfy and warm. The pattern is written for multiple sizes, with instructions on how to customize it to the exact size you desire.

 Featured Yarn

1 (2) skein of Shepherd Bulky from Lorna's Laces (100% superwash merino wool; 4 oz; 140 yds) in color Huron

SKILL LEVEL: Intermediate

SIZE: Cowl (Infinity Scarf)

FINISHED CIRCUMFERENCE:
30 (60)", slightly stretched

FINISHED LENGTH: 8"

MATERIALS

140 (280) yards of bulky-weight yarn ⑤
US size 10 (6.0 mm) circular needle, 16 (32)" cable, or size required for gauge

1 stitch marker
Tapestry needle
Blocking supplies

GAUGE

11 sts and 11 rows = 4" in patt in the round

Gauge is not critical in this patt, but a different gauge will affect yardage and size of cowl.

PATTERN NOTES

Pattern is written for cowl size with infinity scarf size in parentheses. If only one instruction is given, it should be worked for both sizes. Infinity scarf size is shown.

Cowl chart is on page 14. If you prefer to follow written instructions for the charted material, see "Written Instructions for Chart" on page 14.

» MAKE IT YOUR OWN!

As long as you cast on a multiple of 10 stitches, you can create whatever size cowl you want. Remember, adjusting the size will affect the amount of yarn you'll need.

INSTRUCTIONS

CO 80 (160) sts. Join rnd, being careful not to twist. PM to mark beg of rnd.

Ribbing rnd: *K2, P3; rep from * to end of rnd.

Rep ribbing rnd another 3 rnds.

Work chart until piece measures approx 7" from CO edge, ending with rnd 3.

Work ribbing for 4 rnds.

FINISHING

BO loosely in patt. Block cowl to finished measurements given at beg of patt. With tapestry needle, weave in ends.

WRITTEN INSTRUCTIONS FOR CHART

If you prefer to follow written instructions rather than a chart, use the instructions below.

Rnds 1–3: *K7, P3; rep from * to end of rnd.

Rnd 4: Purl all sts.

Rnds 5–7: *K2, P3, K5; rep from * to end of rnd.

Rnd 8: Purl all sts.

Rep rnds 1–8 for patt.

Cyprus Cowl Chart

Repeat = 10 sts

Chart Legend

☐ K

• P

Cyprus Stole

DESIGNED BY THE AUTHOR AND KNIT BY JENNI LESNIAK

As in the Cyprus Cowl, the simple stitch pattern means that this stole looks great on both sides. There's no right or wrong side when it comes to wearing this piece, so there's no need to fuss with it when you throw it on over your outfit in a hurry.

> ### *Featured Yarn*
>
> *4 skeins of Shepherd Worsted from Lorna's Laces (100% superwash merino wool; 4 oz; 225 yds) in color Turquoise*

SKILL LEVEL: Easy

FINISHED MEASUREMENTS:
12" × 72"

MATERIALS

850 yards of worsted-weight
    yarn
US size 8 (5.0 mm) knitting
    needles, or size required
    for gauge
Tapestry needle
Blocking supplies

GAUGE

22 sts and 24 rows = 4" in patt

Gauge is not critical in this patt, but a different gauge will affect yardage and size of scarf.

PATTERN NOTES

Chart is on page 17. If you prefer to follow written instructions for the charted material, see "Written Instructions for Chart" also on page 17.

INSTRUCTIONS

CO 67 sts. Work chart until stole measures approx 67" from CO edge, ending with row 3 or 7.

FINISHING

BO loosely kw (page 92) on WS. Block stole to finished measurements given at beg of patt. With tapestry needle, weave in ends.

Stunning Stitches

WRITTEN INSTRUCTIONS FOR CHART

If you prefer to follow row-by-row written instructions rather than a chart, use the instructions below.

Row 1 (RS): K2, P3, *K7, P3; rep from * to last 2 sts, K2.

Row 2 (WS): K2, *K3, P7; rep from * to last 5 sts, K5.

Row 3: Rep row 1.

Row 4: Knit all sts.

Row 5: K5, *K2, P3, K5; rep from * to last 2 sts, K2.

Row 6: K2, *P5, K3, P2; rep from * to last 5 sts, P3, K2.

Row 7: Rep row 5.

Row 8: Knit all sts.

Rep rows 1–8 for patt.

» Both sides of this stole are stunning. The textured stitch pattern creates a lovely basket weave on the wrong side, as shown above, making this stole completely reversible.

Cyprus Stole Chart

Repeat = 10 sts

Chart Legend

☐ K on RS, P on WS

⊡ P on RS, K on WS

GLARUS TRIO

A beautiful lace panel is the star of the show in the Glarus Trio of accessories. Use a hand-dyed merino-cashmere blend as I did for the ultimate in luxury. With a shawl, a scarf, and a poncho to choose from, you're sure to find the perfect project.

Glarus Poncho

DESIGNED AND KNIT BY THE AUTHOR

Everyone needs a poncho! This piece is started by working a provisional cast on and is then worked flat. The lace panel is worked along one edge, along with a simple but classic I-cord edging. Once the poncho is the desired length, finish both ends with I-cord before seaming.

Featured Yarn

5 (6) skeins of Cricket from Anzula (80% superwash merino, 10% cashmere, 10% nylon; 250 yds) in color Prudence

---

SKILL LEVEL: Intermediate

SIZES: Women's S/M, (L/XL)

FINISHED MEASUREMENTS:
28" wide, 56 (64)" long
(before folding)

MATERIALS

1250 (1500) yards of DK-weight yarn
US size 6 (4.0 mm) circular needle, 24" cable or longer, or size required for gauge
1 stitch marker
Size G (6.0 mm) crochet hook
Waste yarn
Tapestry needle
Blocking supplies

GAUGE

16 sts and 20 rows = 4" in St st

Gauge is not critical in this patt, but a different gauge will affect yardage and size of poncho.

PATTERN NOTES

Chart is on page 23. If you prefer to follow written instructions for the charted material, see "Written Instructions for Chart" on page 21.

Stunning Stitches

INSTRUCTIONS

With waste yarn and crochet hook, ch a minimum of 129 sts.

Set-up row (RS): With knitting needle and yarn for project, PU a total of 129 sts through the back bump of each ch, turn work.

Next Row (WS): Purl all sts.

Poncho

Row 1 (RS): Work row 1 of chart over first 29 sts, PM, knit to end.

Row 2 (WS): Sl 1 wyif, purl to marker, SM, work row 2 of chart to end.

Row 3: Work next row of chart, SM, knit to end.

Row 4: Sl 1 wyif, purl to marker, SM, work next row of chart to end.

Cont working in patt (starting with row 5 of chart), until piece measures approx 50 (58)", ending with row 26.

FINISHING

Work I-Cord BO on RS as follows:

1. K2, K2tog tbl.
2. Sl 3 sts pw back to LH needle.
3. Rep steps 1 and 2 until 3 sts rem. BO all sts.

Carefully undo crochet ch from provisional CO and place live sts (129 sts) onto knitting needle. With WS facing, work I-Cord BO as follows:

1. P2, P2tog.
2. Sl 3 sts pw back to LH needle.
3. Rep steps 1 and 2 until 3 sts rem. BO all sts.

Block poncho to finished measurements given at beg of patt. With tapestry needle, weave in ends.

Using the schematic as a guide, fold the poncho in half as shown with wrong sides together. Using mattress stitch, seam edges together along the slipped-stitch edge, leaving a 12" (or desired width) neck opening.

WRITTEN INSTRUCTIONS FOR CHART

If you prefer to follow row-by-row written instructions rather than a chart, use the instructions below.

Row 1 (RS): Sl 3 wyib, K3, P3, K4, K2tog, K2, YO, K1, YO, K2, ssk, K4, P3.

Row 2 (WS): K3, P3, P2tog tbl, P2, YO, P3, YO, P2, P2tog, P3, K3, P6.

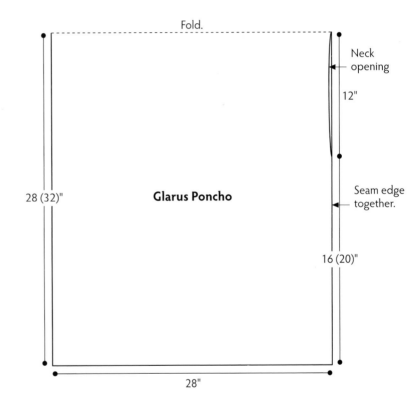

Fold.

Neck opening

12"

28 (32)"

Glarus Poncho

Seam edge together.

16 (20)"

28"

» Use a yarn with subtle color variation to add interest to the body of the poncho.

Row 3: Sl 3 wyib, K3, P3, K2, K2tog, K2, YO, K5, YO, K2, ssk, K2, P3.

Row 4: K3, P1, P2tog tbl, P2, YO, P7, YO, P2, P2tog, P1, K3, P6.

Rows 5–12: Rep rows 1–4 twice.

Row 13: Sl 3 wyib, K3, P3, K1, YO, ssk, YO, K4, sk2p, K4, YO, K2tog, YO, K1, P3.

Rows 14, 16, 18, 20, 22, and 24: K3, P17, K3, P6.

Row 15: Sl 3 wyib, K3, P3, K2, YO, ssk, YO, K3, sk2p, K3, YO, K2tog, YO, K2, P3.

Row 17: Sl 3 wyib, K3, P3, K3, YO, ssk, YO, K2, sk2p, K2, YO, K2tog, YO, K3, P3.

Row 19: Sl 3 wyib, K3, P3, K4, YO, ssk, YO, K1, sk2p, K1, YO, K2tog, YO, K4, P3.

Row 21: Sl 3 wyib, K3, P3, K5, YO, ssk, YO, sk2p, YO, K2tog, YO, K5, P3.

Row 23: Sl 3 wyib, K3, P3, K6, YO, ssk, K1, K2tog, YO, K6, P3.

Row 25: Sl 3 wyib, K3, P3, K7, YO, sk2p, YO, K7, P3.

Row 26: Rep row 14.

Rep rows 1–26 for patt.

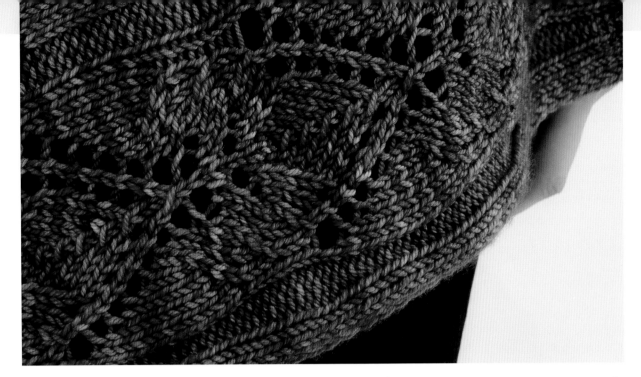

» The I-cord along the edge of the poncho creates a clean, finished look.

Glarus Poncho Chart

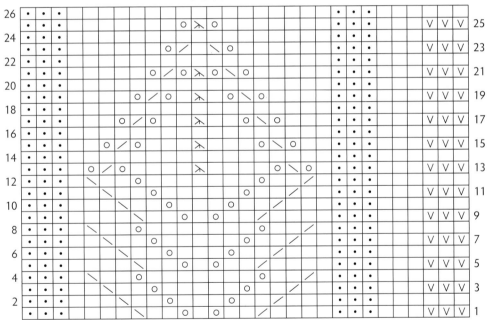

Chart Legend

☐ K on RS, P on WS

• P on RS, K on WS

○ YO

╱ K2tog on RS, P2tog on WS

╲ SSK on RS, P2tog tbl on WS

V Sl 1 wyib on RS

⅄ Sk2p

Stunning Stitches

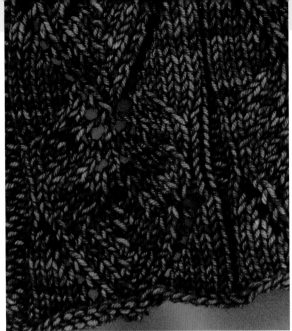

Glarus Scarf

DESIGNED BY THE AUTHOR AND KNIT BY JENNI LESNIAK

Turn up the volume on this stunning lace panel! In the scarf, the panel is worked side by side, creating columns of lace. The pattern is simple to adjust to the size you want, and notes in the instructions tell how you can make it wider or narrower.

 Featured Yarn

3 skeins of For Better or Worsted from Anzula (80% superwash merino, 10% cashmere, 10% nylon; 200 yds) in color Prince

SKILL LEVEL: Intermediate

FINISHED MEASUREMENTS:
10" × 72"

MATERIALS

580 yards of worsted-weight
    yarn (4)
US size 8 (5.0 mm) knitting
    needles, or size required
    for gauge
Tapestry needle
Blocking supplies

GAUGE

20 sts and 28 rows = 4" in St st

Gauge is not critical in this patt, but a different gauge will affect yardage and size of scarf

PATTERN NOTES

Chart is on page 27. If you prefer to follow written instructions for the charted material, see "Written Instructions for Chart" on page 26.

INSTRUCTIONS

CO 46 sts. Work chart until scarf measures approx 68" from CO edge, ending with row 25.

FINISHING

BO loosely kw (page 92) on WS. Block scarf to finished measurements given at beg of patt. With tapestry needle, weave in ends.

> » **MAKE IT YOUR OWN!**
>
> For a wider scarf, cast on an additional 19 stitches (65 stitches total). Want a skinny scarf? Cast on just 27 stitches. Remember, changing the width of your scarf will affect the amount of yarn you need.

WRITTEN INSTRUCTIONS FOR CHART

If you prefer to follow row-by-row written instructions rather than a chart, use the instructions below.

Row 1 (RS): K3, P2, *K4, K2tog, K2, YO, K1, YO, K2, ssk, K4, P2; rep from * to last 3 sts, K3.

Row 2 (WS): K3, *K2, P3, P2tog tbl, P2, YO, P3, YO, P2, P2tog, P3; rep from * to last 5 sts, K5.

Row 3: K3, P2, *K2, K2tog, K2, YO, K5, YO, K2, ssk, K2, P2; rep from * to last 3 sts, K3.

Row 4: K3, *K2, P1, P2tog tbl, P2, YO, P7, YO, P2, P2tog, P1; rep from * to last 5 sts, K5.

Rows 5–12: Rep rows 1–4 twice.

Row 13: K3, P2, *K1, YO, ssk, YO, K4, sk2p, K4, YO, K2tog, YO, K1, P2; rep from * to last 3 sts, K3.

Rows 14, 16, 18, 20, 22, and 24: K3, *K2, P17; rep from * to last 5 sts, K5.

Row 15: K3, P2, *K2, YO, ssk, YO, K3, sk2p, K3, YO, K2tog, YO, K2, P2; rep from * to last 3 sts, K3.

Row 17: K3, P2, *K3, YO, ssk, YO, K2, sk2p, K2, YO, K2tog, YO, K3, P2; rep from * to last 3 sts, K3.

Row 19: K3, P2, *K4, YO, ssk, YO, K1, sk2p, K1, YO, K2tog, YO, K4, P2; rep from * to last 3 sts, K3.

Row 21: K3, P2, *K5, YO, ssk, YO, sk2p, YO, K2tog, YO, K5, P2; rep from * to last 3 sts, K3.

Row 23: K3, P2, *K6, YO, ssk, K1, K2tog, YO, K6, P2; rep from * to last 3 sts, K3.

Row 25: K3, P2, *K7, YO, sk2p, YO, K7, P2; rep from * to last 3 sts, K3.

Row 26: Rep row 14.

Rep rows 1–26 for patt.

Glarus Scarf Chart

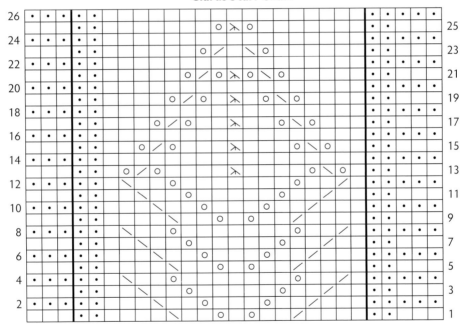

Repeat = 19 sts

Chart Legend

☐ K on RS, P on WS   ╱ K2tog on RS, P2tog on WS

• P on RS, K on WS   ╲ SSK on RS, P2tog tbl on WS

○ YO   ⋋ Sk2p

Stunning Stitches

Glarus Shawl

DESIGNED BY THE AUTHOR AND KNIT BY CATHY RUSK

For this elegant shawl, the lace panel is used as a knitted-on border. A gorgeous leaf-shaped lace is worked in the body of the piece to complement the panel pattern.

Featured Yarn

1 skein of Cloud from Anzula (80% superwash merino; 10% cashmere, 10% nylon; 575 yds), in color Lapis

---

SKILL LEVEL: Intermediate

FINISHED MEASUREMENTS:
76" × 21"

MATERIALS

575 yards of fingering-weight yarn
US size 5 (3.75 mm) circular needle, 24" or longer, or size required for gauge
Tapestry needle
Blocking supplies

GAUGE

20 sts and 28 rows = 4" in St st

Gauge is not critical in this patt, but a different gauge will affect yardage and size of shawl.

PATTERN NOTES

Chart A is on page 32 and chart B is on page 31. If you prefer to follow written instructions for the charted material, see "Written Instructions for Charts" on page 30.

INSTRUCTIONS

Work garter tab CO (page 92) as follows: CO 2 sts. Knit 14 rows. Turn work 90° and pick up 7 sts along the edge. Turn work 90° and pick up 2 sts from CO edge— 11 sts total.

Set-up row (WS): Knit all sts.

Row 1 (RS): K2, (YO, K1) 7 times, YO, K2—19 sts.

Row 2: K2, purl to the last 2 sts, K2.

BODY OF SHAWL

Work chart A 5 times. Work rows 1–19 of chart A once more—305 sts.

Next row (WS): K3, YO, K1, K2tog twice, knit to the last 8 sts, K2tog twice, K1, YO, K3—302 sts.

STITCH COUNT FOR BODY OF SHAWL	
Rep 1 of chart A	67 sts
Rep 2 of chart A	115 sts
Rep 3 of chart A	163 sts
Rep 4 of chart A	211 sts
Rep 5 of chart A	259 sts
Rows 1–19 of chart A	305 sts
Final WS row	302 sts

LACE EDGING

With RS facing, CO 25 sts using the knitted CO.

First Border

Row 1 (RS): K24, ssk last border st with first body st on left needle.

Row 2 (WS): Sl 1 wyib, K24. Rep rows 1 and 2 once more.

Edge Chart

Work chart B 23 times.

Final Border

Row 1 (RS): K24, ssk last border st with first body st on left needle.

Row 2 (WS): Sl 1 wyib, K24. Rep row 1 once more.

FINISHING

BO loosely kw (page 92) on WS. Block shawl to finished measurements given at beg of patt. With tapestry needle, weave in ends.

WRITTEN INSTRUCTIONS FOR CHARTS

If you prefer to follow row-by-row written instructions rather than a chart, use the instructions below.

Chart A

Row 1 (RS): K2, YO, K2, *YO, ssk, K7, K2tog, YO, K1; rep from * to last 3 sts, K1, YO, K2.

Row 2 and all even-numbered rows (WS): K3, YO, K1, purl to the last 4 sts, K1, YO, K3.

Row 3: K2, YO, K4, *K1, YO, ssk, K5, K2tog, YO, K2; rep from * to last 5 sts, K3, YO, K2.

Row 5: (K2, YO) twice, ssk, K2, *K2, YO, ssk, K3, K2tog, YO, K3; rep from * to last 7 sts, K1, K2tog, (YO, K2) twice.

Row 7: K2, YO, K5, *YO, ssk, K1, K2tog, YO, K1; rep from * to last 6 sts, K4, YO, K2.

Row 9: K2, YO, K3, YO, ssk, K3, YO, sk2p, *YO, K3, YO, sk2p; rep from * to last 10 sts, YO, K3, K2tog, YO, K3, YO, K2.

Row 11: K2, YO, *K3, K2tog, YO, K1, YO, ssk, K4; rep from * to last 13 sts, K3, K2tog, YO, K1, YO, ssk, K3, YO, K2.

Row 13: (K2, YO) twice, *K2, K2tog, YO, K3, YO, ssk, K3; rep from * to last 15 sts, K2, K2tog, YO, K3, YO, ssk, (K2, YO) twice, K2.

Row 15: (K2, YO) twice, K3, *K1, K2tog, YO, K5, YO, ssk, K2; rep from * to last 6 sts, (K2, YO) twice, K2.

Row 17: (K2, YO) twice, *K2tog, YO, K1, YO, ssk, K1; rep from * to last 9 sts, K2tog, YO, K1, YO, ssk, (YO, K2) twice.

Row 19: K2, YO, K4, YO, K2tog, *YO, K3, YO, sk2p; rep from * to last 11 sts, YO, K3, YO, ssk, YO, K4, YO, K2.

Row 20: K3, YO, K1, purl to the last 4 sts, K1, YO, K3.

Rep rows 1–20 for patt.

Chart B

Row 1 (RS): K3, P1, K4, K2tog, K2, YO, K1, YO, K2, ssk, K4, P1, K2, ssk last border st with next body st on left needle.

Row 2 (WS): Sl 1 wyib, K3, P3, P2tog tbl, P2, YO, P3, YO, P2, P2tog, P3, K4.

Row 3: K3, P1, K2, K2tog, K2, YO, K5, YO, K2, ssk, K2, P1, K2, ssk last border st with next body st on left needle.

Row 4: Sl 1 wyib, K3, P1, P2tog tbl, P2, YO, P7, YO, P2, P2tog, P1, K4.

Rows 5–12: Rep rows 1–4 twice.

Row 13: K3, P1, K1, YO, ssk, YO, K4, sk2p, K4, YO, K2tog, YO, K1, P1, K2, ssk last border st with next body st on left needle.

Rows 14, 16, 18, 20, 22, and 24: Sl 1 wyib, K3, P17, K4.

Row 15: K3, P1, K2, YO, ssk, YO, K3, sk2p, K3, YO, K2tog, YO, K2, P1, K2, ssk last border st with next body st on left needle.

Row 17: K3, P1, K3, YO, ssk, YO, K2, sk2p, K2, YO, K2tog, YO, K3, P1, K2, ssk last border st with next body st on left needle.

Row 19: K3, P1, K4, YO, ssk, YO, K1, sk2p, K1, YO, K2tog, YO, K4, P1, K2, ssk last border st with next body st on left needle.

Row 21: K3, P1, K5, YO, ssk, YO, sk2p, YO, K2tog, YO, K5, P1, K2, ssk last border st with next body st on left needle.

Row 23: K3, P1, K6, YO, ssk, K1, K2tog, YO, K6, P1, K2, ssk last border st with next body st on left needle.

Row 25: K3, P1, K7, YO, sk2p, YO, K7, P1, K2, ssk last border st with next body st on left needle.

Row 26: Rep row 14.

Rep rows 1–26 for patt.

Please note that this is chart B, and that chart A can be found on page 32.

Glarus Shawl Chart B

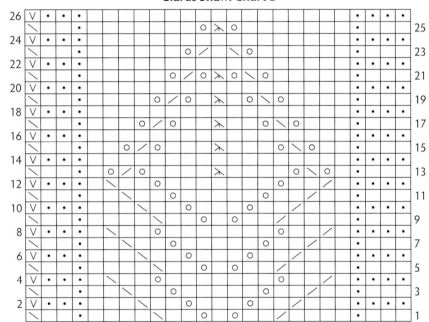

Chart Legend

☐ K on RS, P on WS

⊡ P on RS, K on WS

○ YO

╲ SSK on RS, P2tog tbl on WS

Ⅴ Sl 1 wyib on WS

ⅹ Sk2p

Glarus Shawl Chart A

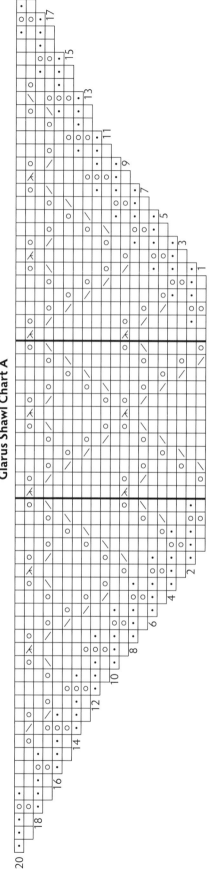

Repeat = 12 sts

Chart Legend

☐ K on RS, P on WS	◻ K2tog	
• P on RS, K on WS	◻ SSK	
○ YO	☒ Sk2p	

KELSEY TRIO

A sweet cable with garter-stitch detail adorns the Kelsey Trio. To show off the design, pair any of the patterns with a soft and squishy yarn that provides great stitch definition. With a hooded scarf, a shawl, and a cowl to choose from, you'll be both warm and stylish all winter long.

Stunning Stitches

Kelsey Hooded Scarf

DESIGNED AND KNIT BY THE AUTHOR

Living in the Midwest, I'm not sure how a hooded scarf has been missing from my wardrobe until now! This fun accessory combines the warmth of a hat with the versatility of a scarf and can be worn in a variety of ways.

Featured Yarn

2 skeins of Yellowstone from Stitch Sprouts (80% wool, 20% silk; 100 g; 285 yds) in color Old Faithful

SKILL LEVEL: Experienced

FINISHED MEASUREMENTS:
10" center back to edge of hood;
12½" neck to top of hood;
84" scarf length

MATERIALS

510 yards of sport weight yarn
US size 6 (4.0 mm) knitting needles, or size required for gauge

Cable needle
1 stitch marker
Tapestry needle
Blocking supplies

GAUGE

22 sts and 24 rows = 4" in garter st

Gauge is not critical in this patt, but a different gauge will affect yardage and size of scarf.

PATTERN NOTES

When binding off 45 stitches at the end of the hood section, there's 1 stitch on the right-hand needle. This counts as the first stitch of the K4 that follows the binding off.

Charts are on pages 37 and 38. If you prefer to follow written instructions for the charted material, see "Written Instructions for Charts" on page 37.

» The cable pattern travels along the edges of the scarf and also adorns the hood to elegantly frame your face.

SPECIAL ABBREVIATIONS

2/2 RC: Sl 2 sts to cn, hold in back, K2, K2 from cn

2/2 LC: Sl 2 sts to cn, hold in front, K2, K2 from cn

2/1 RPC: Sl 1 st to cn, hold in back, K2, P1 from cn

2/1 LPC: Sl 2 sts to cn, hold in front, P1, K2 from cn

INSTRUCTIONS

CO 28 sts.

Foundation row (WS): Knit.

Row 1 (RS): K14, PM, knit to end.

Row 2 (WS): Knit to marker, SM, P2, K8, P2, K2.

Row 3: K14, SM, work row 1 of chart A to end.

Row 4: Work row 2 of chart A to marker, SM, K14.

Row 5: K14, SM, work row 3 of chart A to end.

Row 6: Work row 4 of chart A to marker, SM, K14.

Cont in est patt, (working garter st [K every row] on one side of marker and working next row of chart A, starting with row 5), until chart A has been repeated a total of 11 times. Cont in est patt for 12 more rows (ending with row 12 of chart A).

Next row (RS): K14, SM, work row 13 of chart A to end.

With WS facing, CO 45 sts using knitted CO—73 sts total.

Next row (WS): P1, K48, P8, K2, SM, knit to end.

Next row (RS): K14, SM, P2, K8, (P3, K8) 4 times, P2, K3.

Next row (WS): P1, K4, (P8, K3) 4 times, P8, K2, SM, knit to end.

Cont in est patt, (working garter st on one side of marker and working next row of chart B, starting with row 1), until chart B has been repeated a total of 8 times. Cont in est patt for 9 more rows (ending with row 9 of chart B).

Next row (WS): BO 45 sts, K4, P8, K2, SM, knit to end (28 sts).

Stunning Stitches

Cont in est patt, (working garter st on one side of marker and working next row of chart A, starting with row 11), until chart A has been completed once (6 rows).

Cont in est patt until chart A has been worked another 11 times. Cont in est patt for 9 more rows (ending with row 9 of chart A).

Final row (WS): Knit all sts, removing marker.

FINISHING

BO loosely kw (page 92) on RS. Block scarf to finished measurements given at beg of patt. With tapestry needle, weave in ends.

Using schematic as a guide, fold hooded scarf in half as shown with wrong sides together.

Using mattress stitch, seam edges together on top of hood. Weave in remaining ends.

WRITTEN INSTRUCTIONS FOR CHARTS

If you prefer to follow row-by-row written instructions rather than a chart, use the instructions below.

Kelsey Hooded Scarf Chart A

Row 1 (RS): P2, 2/2 RC, 2/2 LC, P2, K2.

Row 2 (WS): K4, P8, K2.

Row 3: P1, 2/1 RPC, P4, 2/1 LPC, P1, K2.

Row 4: K3, P10, K1.

Row 5: P1, K2, P6, K2, P1, K2.

Row 6: Rep row 4.

Row 7: P1, 2/1 LPC, P4, 2/1 RPC, P1, K2.

Row 8: Rep row 2.

Row 9: Rep row 1.

Row 10: Rep row 2.

Row 11: P2, K8, P2, K2.

Rows 12–15: Rep rows 8–11.

Row 16: Rep row 2.

Rep rows 1–16 for patt.

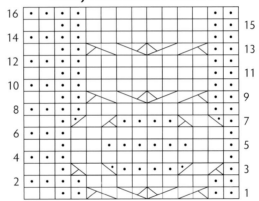

Kelsey Hooded Scarf Chart A

Chart Legend

☐ K on RS, P on WS		◿◺ 2/1 LPC	
• P on RS, K on WS		⬚⬚ 2/2 RC	
◺◿ 2/1 RPC		⬚⬚ 2/2 LC	

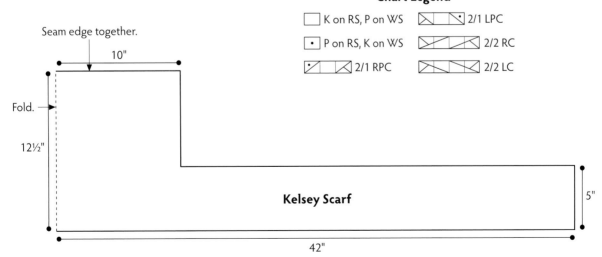

Seam edge together.

10"

Fold.

12½"

Kelsey Scarf

42"

5"

Kelsey Hooded Scarf Chart B

Row 1 (RS): P2, *2/2 RC, 2/2 LC, P3; rep from * to last 13 sts, 2/2 RC, 2/2 LC, P2, K3.

Row 2 (WS): P1, K4, *P8, K3; rep from * to last 10 sts, P8, K2.

Row 3: P1, 2/1 RPC, P4, 2/1 LPC, P1, *P1, K8, P2, 2/1 RPC, P4, 2/1 LPC, P1; rep from * to last 3 sts, K3.

Row 4: P1, K2, *K1, P10, K2, P8, K1; rep from * to last 12 sts, K1, P10, K1.

Row 5: P1, K2, P6, K2, P1, *P1, 2/2 RC, 2/2 LC, P2, K2, P6, K2, P1; rep from * to last 3 sts, K3.

Row 6: Rep row 4.

Row 7: P1, 2/1 LPC, P4, 2/1 RPC, P1, *P1, K8, P2, 2/1 LPC, P4, 2/1 RPC, P1; rep from * to last 3 sts, K3.

Row 8: Rep row 2.

Row 9: Rep row 1.

Row 10: Rep row 2.

Row 11: P2, K8, P2, *2/1 RPC, P4, 2/1 LPC, P2, K8, P2; rep from * to last 3 sts, K3.

Row 12: P1, K2, *K2, P8, K2, P10; rep from * to last 12 sts, K2, P8, K2.

Row 13: P2, 2/2 RC, 2/2 LC, P2, *K2, P6, K2, P2, 2/2 RC, 2/2 LC, P2; rep from * to last 3 sts, K3.

Row 14: Rep row 12.

Row 15: P2, K8, P2, *2/1 LPC, P4, 2/1 RPC, P2, K8, P2; rep from * to last 3 sts, K3.

Row 16: Rep row 2.

Rep rows 1–16 for patt.

Kelsey Hooded Scarf Chart B

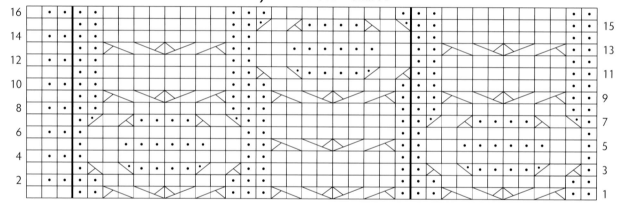

Repeat = 22 sts

Chart Legend

☐ K on RS, P on WS	⬔ 2/1 LPC
⊡ P on RS, K on WS	⬔ 2/2 RC
⬔ 2/1 RPC	⬔ 2/2 LC

Kelsey Cowl

DESIGNED AND KNIT BY THE AUTHOR

Offset cables add a twist to the cable-and-garter stitch pattern. The pattern is written for two sizes, so you can make either a cowl that you can keep close to your neck or a larger infinity scarf, which you can wear doubled for extra warmth.

> ### Featured Yarn
> *2 (3) skeins of Crater Lake from Stitch Sprouts (100% superwash merino; 100 g; 110 yds) in color Wizard Island*

SKILL LEVEL: Intermediate

SIZE: Cowl (Infinity Scarf)

FINISHED CIRCUMFERENCE:
24 (48)" slightly stretched

FINISHED LENGTH: 8"

MATERIALS

160 (320) yards of bulky-weight yarn
US size 10 (6.0 mm) circular needle, 16 (32)", or size required for gauge

1 stitch marker
Cable needle
Tapestry needle
Blocking supplies

GAUGE

16 sts and 20 rows = 4" in cable patt in the round

Gauge is not critical in this patt, but a different gauge will affect yardage and size of cowl.

PATTERN NOTES

Pattern is written for cowl size with infinity scarf size in parentheses. If only one instruction is given, it should be worked for both sizes. Cowl size is shown.

Cowl chart is on page 41. If you prefer to follow written instructions for the charted material, see "Written Instructions for Chart" on page 41.

Stunning Stitches

SPECIAL ABBREVIATIONS

2/2 RC: Sl 2 sts to cn, hold in back, K2, K2 from cn

2/2 LC: Sl 2 sts to cn, hold in front, K2, K2 from cn

2/1 RPC: Sl 1 st to cn, hold in back, K2, P1 from cn

2/1 LPC: Sl 2 sts to cn, hold in front, P1, K2 from cn

INSTRUCTIONS

CO 88 (176) sts. Join rnd being careful not to twist. PM to mark beg of rnd.

Set-up rnd: P1, *K8, P3; rep from * to last 10 sts, K8, P2.

Work rnds 1–16 of cowl chart 3 times (48 rnds total). Work rnds 1 and 2 of cowl chart once more.

FINISHING

BO loosely in patt. Block cowl to finished measurements given at beg of patt. With tapestry needle, weave in ends.

WRITTEN INSTRUCTIONS FOR CHART

If you prefer to follow row-by-row written instructions rather than a chart, use the instructions below.

Rnd 1: *P1, 2/2 RC, 2/2 LC, P3, 2/2 RC, 2/2 LC, P2; rep from * to end of rnd.

Rnd 2: *P1, K8, P3, K8, P2; rep from * to end of rnd.

Rnd 3: *P1, K8, P2, 2/1 RPC, P4, 2/1 LPC, P1; rep from * to end of rnd.

» MAKE IT YOUR OWN!

As long as you cast on a multiple of 22 stitches, you can create whatever size cowl you want. Because this pattern is so easy to adjust, it's perfect for experimenting with different weights of yarn. Remember, adjusting the size will affect the amount of yarn you'll need.

Rnd 4: *P1, K8, P2, K10, P1; rep from * to end of rnd.

Rnd 5: *P1, 2/2 RC, 2/2 LC, P2, K2, P6, K2, P1; rep from * to end of rnd.

Rnd 6: Rep rnd 4.

Rnd 7: *P1, K8, P2, 2/1 LPC, P4, 2/1 RPC, P1; rep from * to end of rnd.

Rnd 8: Rep rnd 2.

Rnd 9: Rep rnd 1.

Rnd 10: Rep rnd 2.

Rnd 11: *2/1 RPC, P4, 2/1 LPC, P2, K8, P2; rep from * to end of rnd.

Rnd 12: *K10, P2, K8, P2; rep from * to end of rnd.

Rnd 13: *K2, P6, K2, P2, 2/2 RC, 2/2 LC, P2; rep from * to end of rnd.

Rnd 14: Rep rnd 12.

Rnd 15: *2/1 LPC, P4, 2/1 RPC, P2, K8, P2; rep from * to end of rnd.

Rnd 16: Rep rnd 2.

Rep rnds 1–16 for patt.

Kelsey Cowl Chart

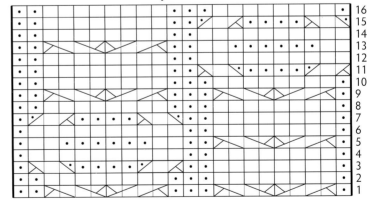

Repeat = 22 sts

Chart Legend

	K		2/1 LPC
	P		2/2 RC
	2/1 RPC		2/2 LC

Stunning Stitches

Kelsey Shawl

DESIGNED AND KNIT BY THE AUTHOR

An asymmetrical garter stitch shawl offers the ideal shape and texture to show off this cable-and-garter stitch pattern. Small bobbles accent the edge for extra texture.

Featured Yarn

2 skeins of Yellowstone from Stitch Sprouts (80% wool, 20% silk; 100 g; 285 yds) in color Reese Creek

---

SKILL LEVEL: Experienced

FINISHED MEASUREMENTS: 22" × 70"

MATERIALS

560 yards of sport-weight yarn (2)

US size 5 (3.75 mm) circular needle, 24" or longer, or size required for gauge

1 stitch marker

Cable needle

Tapestry needle

Blocking supplies

GAUGE

20 sts and 32 rows = 4" in garter st

Gauge is not critical in this patt, but a different gauge will affect yardage and size of shawl.

PATTERN NOTES

Charts are on page 45. If you prefer to follow written instructions for the charted material, see "Written Instructions for Charts" on page 44.

SPECIAL ABBREVIATIONS

2/2 RC: Sl 2 sts to cn, hold in back. K2, K2 from cn.

2/2 LC: Sl 2 sts to cn, hold in front, K2, K2 from cn.

2/1 RPC: Sl 1 st to cn, hold in back, K2, P1 from cn.

2/1 LPC: Sl 2 sts to cn, hold in front, P1, K2 from cn.

MB: Make bobble, work as follows: (K1, P1) 3 times into st, sl first 5 sts on RH needle over 6th st.

» MAKE IT YOUR OWN!

Want a bigger shawl? You can have one! Repeat rows 5 and 6 of the "body of shawl" section until you've worked chart A an odd number of times (15, 17, 19, and so on, total). Then work the last 7 rows of the body and lace-border sections as written. Don't forget—if you make your shawl bigger, you'll need more yarn!

» Bobbles along the edge of the cable panel create texture at the edge of the shawl.

INSTRUCTIONS

CO 25 sts.

Knit 1 row on WS.

Body of Shawl

Row 1 (RS): K1, K1f&b, K1, K2tog, K1, PM, K19.

Row 2 (WS): K19, SM, knit to 2 sts before end, K1f&b, K1—26 sts.

Row 3: K1, K1f&b, knit to 3 sts before marker, K2tog, K1, SM, work row 1 of chart A to end.

Row 4: Work row 2 of chart A to marker, SM, knit to last 2 sts, K1f&b, K1—1 st inc in garter st section.

Row 5: K1, K1f&b, knit to 3 sts before marker, K2tog, K1, SM, work next row of chart A to end.

Row 6: Work next row of chart A to marker, SM, knit to last 2 sts, K1f&b, K1—1 st inc in garter st section.

Work rows 5 and 6 of body of shawl (working next row of chart A, starting with row 5) another 118 times (chart A will be worked a total of 15 times). (146 sts—127 in garter st section, 19 sts for chart A)

Cont in est patt for another 7 rows (149 sts—130 sts in garter st section, 19 sts for chart A).

Next row (WS): Knit to marker, remove marker, knit to last 2 sts, K1f&b, K1—150 sts.

Lace Border

CO 7 sts using knitted CO. Work chart B 74 times. Work rows 1–3 of chart B once more.

FINISHING

BO rem sts on WS. Block shawl to finished measurements given at beg of patt. With tapestry needle, weave in ends.

WRITTEN INSTRUCTIONS FOR CHARTS

If you prefer to follow row-by-row written instructions rather than a chart, use the instructions below.

Chart A

Row 1 (RS): K1, K2tog, YO, K2, P2, 2/2 RC, 2/2 LC, P2, K2.

Row 2 (WS): MB, K3, P8, K2, K2tog, YO, K3.

Row 3: K1, K2tog, YO, K2, P1, 2/1 RPC, P4, 2/1 LPC, P1, K2.

Row 4: K3, P10, K1, K2tog, YO, K3.

Row 5: K1, K2tog, YO, K2, P1, K2, P6, K2, P1, K2.

Row 6: MB, K2, P10, K1, K2tog, YO, K3.

Row 7: K1, K2tog, YO, K2, P1, 2/1 LPC, P4, 2/1 RPC, P1, K2.

Row 8: K4, P8, K2, K2tog, YO, K3.

Row 9: Rep row 1.

Row 10: Rep row 2.

Row 11: K1, K2tog, YO, K2, P2, K8, P2, K2.

Rows 12–15: Rep rows 8–11.

Row 16: Rep row 8.

Rep rows 1–16 for patt.

Chart B

Row 1 (RS): MB, K1, K2tog, YO, K2, ssk last border st with next body st on left needle.

Row 2 (WS): Sl 1 wyib, K2tog, YO, K4.

Row 3: K2, K2tog, YO, K2, ssk the last border st with next body st on left needle.

Row 4: Rep row 2.

Rep rows 1–4 for patt.

» TAKE NOTE

K2tog on WS is as simple as it sounds: Just work a normal K2tog on the wrong side of your work! It has its own symbol in the chart because traditionally when the K2tog stitch is worked on the WS, it's done as a P2tog. However, because you're working in garter stitch for this shawl, you need to do a regular K2tog on the WS.

Kelsey Shawl Chart A

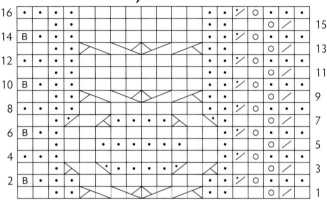

Kelsey Shawl Chart B

Chart Legend

☐ K on RS, P on WS	Ⅴ Sl 1 wyib on WS	
• P on RS, K on WS	B MB	
○ YO	☑ ☒	2/1 RPC
◢ K2tog on RS	◣ ◢	2/1 LPC
☑ K2tog on WS	◣◢ ◣◢	2/2 RC
◣ SSK	◢◣ ◢◣	2/2 LC

BAMPTON TRIO

Lace with garter stitch detailing adorns the beautiful Bampton Trio accessories. The lace creates a small chevron effect, which highlights the lovely color changes of a sumptuous gradient-effect yarn. This set features a cowlette, cowl, and shawl—all are quick to knit!

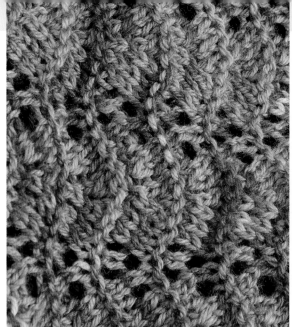

Bampton Cowl

DESIGNED AND KNIT BY THE AUTHOR

I love any lace pattern that creates a feather-and-fan effect, and with this cowl, the lace is the star. The cowl size is very easy to adjust, which means you can create the exact cowl or infinity scarf you want.

Yarn Used for Featured Cowl

1 skein of Posh Panda from Yarn in the Box (60% superwash merino, 30% bamboo, 10% nylon; 4 oz; 434 yds) in color Copper Pennies

SKILL LEVEL: Easy

SIZE: Cowl (Infinity Scarf)

FINISHED CIRCUMFERENCE:
36 (72)", slightly stretched

FINISHED LENGTH: 10"

MATERIALS

270 (540) yards of sport-weight yarn

US size 4 (3.5 mm) circular needle, 16 (32)" cable, or size required for gauge

1 stitch marker

Tapestry needle

Blocking supplies

GAUGE

16 sts and 32 rows = 4" in cowl chart patt in the round

Gauge is not critical in this patt, but a different gauge will affect yardage and size of cowl.

PATTERN NOTES

Pattern is written for cowl size with infinity scarf size in parentheses. If only one instruction is given, it should be worked for both sizes. Cowl size is shown.

Stunning Stitches

Cowl chart is below right. If you prefer to follow written instructions for the charted material, see "Written Instructions for Chart" below.

INSTRUCTIONS

CO 144 (288) sts. Join rnd being careful not to twist. PM to mark beg of rnd.

Set-up rnd 1: Purl all sts.

Set-up rnd 2: Knit all sts.

Work rnds 1–6 of cowl chart 12 times (72 rnds total). Work rnds 1–5 of cowl chart once more.

FINISHING

BO loosely kw (page 92). Block cowl to finished measurements given at beg of patt. With tapestry needle, weave in ends.

WRITTEN INSTRUCTIONS FOR CHART

If you prefer to follow row-by-row written instructions rather than a chart, use the instructions below.

Rnd 1: *K1, YO, K2, ssk, K2tog, K2, YO; rep from * to end.

Rnd 2 and all even-numbered rnds: Knit all sts.

Rnd 3: *YO, K2, ssk, K2tog, K2, YO, K1; rep from * to end.

Rnd 5: Purl all sts.

Rnd 6: Knit all sts.

Rep rnds 1–6 for patt.

> **» MAKE IT YOUR OWN!**
>
> Cast on any multiple of nine stitches to create whatever size cowl you want. Remember, adjusting the size will affect the amount of yarn you'll need.

Bampton Cowl Chart

•	•	•	•	•	•	•	•	•		6 5
										4
	○			╱	╲			○		3 2
○			╱	╲			○			1

Repeat = 9 sts

Chart Legend

☐ K   ╱ K2tog

• P   ╲ SSK

○ YO

Stunning Stitches

Bampton Cowlette

DESIGNED AND KNIT BY THE AUTHOR

I love triangle shawls, but I admit that sometimes they're difficult to keep in place when you wear them. This cowlette solves that problem—it's a triangle shawl that you transform into a cowl! Work the simple triangle back and forth, and then join the piece in the round and add the lace. It's fun to knit, and your shawl won't slip off your shoulders!

> ### Featured Yarn
> *1 skein of Gradient DK Weight from Done Roving Yarns (100% superwash merino; 4 oz, 350 yds) in color 20 Red Maple Grove*

SKILL LEVEL: Intermediate

FINISHED MEASUREMENTS:
28" neck circumference; 20" long in front, and 7" long in back

MATERIALS

300 yards of DK-weight yarn
US size 5 (3.75 mm) circular
   needle, 24" cable, or size
   required for gauge
5 stitch markers
Tapestry needle
Blocking supplies

GAUGE

22 sts and 28 rows = 4" in St st

PATTERN NOTES

Chart is on page 53. If you prefer to follow written instructions for the charted material, see "Written Instructions for Chart" on page 52.

This pattern calls for five stitch markers. You may find it helpful to use four markers of one color and the final marker of another color. This fifth stitch marker will be used to indicate the start of the round.

INSTRUCTIONS

Work garter-tab CO (page 92) as follows: CO 2 sts. Knit 14 rows. Turn work 90° and pick up 7 sts along the edge. Turn work 90° and pick up 2 sts from CO edge— 11 sts total.

STITCH COUNT FOR LACE SECTION	
Rep 1 of chart	171 sts
Rep 2 of chart	207 sts
Rnds 1–5 of chart	219 sts

FINISHING

BO loosely kw (page 92).

Block cowlette to finished measurements given at beg of patt. With tapestry needle, weave in ends.

WRITTEN INSTRUCTIONS FOR CHART

If you prefer to follow row-by-row written instructions rather than a chart, use the instructions below.

Rnd 1: K2, SM, YO, K1, *K1, YO, K2, ssk, K2tog, K2, YO; rep from * to 1 st before marker, K1, YO, SM, K1, SM, YO, K1, **YO, K2, ssk, K2tog, K2, YO, K1; rep from ** to 1 st before marker, K1, YO, SM, K2.

Rnd 2 and all even-numbered rnds: P2, knit to the last 2 sts, P2.

Rnd 3: K2, SM, YO, K2, *YO, K2, ssk, K2tog, K2, YO, K1; rep from * to 2 sts before marker, K2, YO, SM, K1, SM, YO, K2, **K1, YO, K2, ssk, K2tog, K2, YO; rep from ** to 2 sts before marker, K2, YO, SM, K2.

Rnd 5: K2, SM, YO, K1, purl to marker, YO, SM, P1, SM, YO, purl to 1 st before marker, K1, YO, SM, K2.

» By first working back and forth in rows and then joining in the round, you create a piece that is longer in the front and shorter in the back. It's a triangle shawl that can't fall off!

Stockinette Section (In rows)

Set-up row (WS): K2, PM, P3, PM, P1, PM, P3, PM, K2.

Row 1 (RS): K2, SM, YO, knit to next marker, YO, SM, K1, SM, YO, knit to last marker, YO, SM, K2 (15 sts).

Row 2 (WS): K2, purl to last 2 sts, K2.

Work rows 1 and 2 another 29 times (30 times total; 131 sts).

Rep row 1 once more—135 sts.

Do not turn work. You'll now be working in the round. Join rnd, being careful not to twist. PM to mark beg of rnd.

Lace Section (In the Round)

Set-up rnd: P2, knit to last 2 sts, P2.

Work cowlette chart 2 times.

Work rnds 1–5 of cowlette chart once more.

Rnd 7: K2, SM, YO, K4, *K1, YO, K2, ssk, K2tog, K2, YO; rep from * to 4 sts before marker, K4, YO, SM, K1, SM, YO, K4, **YO, K2, ssk, K2tog, K2, YO, K1; rep from ** to 4 sts before marker, K4, YO, SM, K2.

Rnd 9: K2, YO, K5, *YO, K2, ssk, K2tog, K2, YO, K1; rep from * to 5 sts before marker, K5, YO, SM, K1, SM, YO, K5, **K1, YO, K2, ssk, K2tog, K2, YO; rep from ** to 5 sts before marker, K5, YO, SM, K2.

Rnd 11: Rep rnd 5.

Rnd 13: K2, SM, YO, K3, K2tog, K2, YO, *K1, YO, K2, ssk, K2tog, K2, YO; rep from * to 7 sts before marker, K1, YO, K2, ssk, K2, YO, SM, K1, SM, YO, K2, K2tog, K2, YO, K1, **YO, K2, ssk, K2tog, K2, YO, K1; rep from ** to 7 sts before marker, YO, K2, ssk, K3, YO, SM, K2.

Rnd 15: K2, SM, YO, K3, K2tog, K2, YO, K1, *YO, K2, ssk, K2tog, K2, YO, K1; rep from * to 8 sts before marker, YO, K2, ssk, K4, YO, SM, K1, SM, YO, K4, K2tog, K2, YO, **K1, YO, K2, ssk, K2tog, K2, YO; rep from ** to 8 sts before marker, K1, YO, K2, ssk, K3, YO, SM, K2.

Rnd 17: Rep rnd 5.

Rnd 18: P2, knit to the last 2 sts, P2.

Rep rnds 1–18 for patt.

Chart Legend

☐ K	⟍ K2tog
• P	⟋ SSK
○ YO	▨ No stitch

Bampton Cowlette Chart

Repeat = 9 sts

Repeat = 9 sts

Stunning Stitches

Bampton Shawl

DESIGNED AND KNIT BY THE AUTHOR

Here's the perfect project for a vivid gradient-effect yarn. The chevron lace pattern creates interesting texture, and the lace looks lovely in a variety of colors. The yarn I chose adds to the drama, as a single ball contains four complementary colorways.

Yarn Used for Featured Shawl

1 skein of Frolicking Feet Transitions from Done Roving Yarns (100% domestic superwash merino; 4 oz; 480 yds) in color 26 Downton Masterpiece

SKILL LEVEL: Intermediate

FINISHED MEASUREMENTS: 52" × 27"

MATERIALS

475 yards of fingering-weight yarn (1)
US size 5 (3.75 mm) circular needle, 24" cable, or size required for gauge
4 stitch markers
Tapestry needle
Blocking supplies

GAUGE

16 sts and 20 rows = 4" in St st

Gauge is not critical in this patt, but a different gauge will affect yardage and size of shawl.

PATTERN NOTES

Chart is on page 57. If you prefer to follow written instructions for the charted material, see "Written Instructions for Chart" on page 56.

INSTRUCTIONS

Work garter-tab CO (page 92) as follows: CO 2 sts. Knit 14 rows. Turn work 90° and pick up 7 sts along the edge. Turn work 90° and pick up 2 sts from CO edge— 11 sts total.

Set-up row (WS): K2, PM, K3, PM, K1, PM, K3, PM, K2.

Row 1 (RS): K2, SM, YO, K3, YO, SM, K1, SM, YO, K3, YO, SM, K2— 15 sts.

» This shawl was stitched in Done Roving's Frolicking Feet Transitions yarn. With just one ball of yarn, you can create a shawl that contains four complementary colorways. The yarn comes prewound into a cake and the sample was worked by starting from the inside of the yarn cake.

FINISHING

BO loosely kw (page 92). Block shawl to finished measurements given at beg of patt. With tapestry needle, weave in ends.

WRITTEN INSTRUCTIONS FOR CHART

If you prefer to follow row-by-row written instructions rather than a chart, use the instructions below.

Row 1: K2, SM, YO, K1, *K1, YO, K2, ssk, K2tog, K2, YO; rep from * to 1 st before marker, K1, YO, SM, K1, SM, YO, K1, **YO, K2, ssk, K2tog, K2, YO, K1; rep from ** to 1 st before marker, K1, YO, SM, K2.

Row 2 and all even-numbered rows: K2, purl to last 2 sts, K2.

Row 3: K2, SM, YO, K2, *YO, K2, ssk, K2tog, K2, YO, K1; rep from * to 2 sts before marker, K2, YO, SM, K1, SM, YO, K2, **K1, YO, K2, ssk, K2tog, K2, YO; rep from ** to 2 sts before marker, K2, YO, SM, K2.

Row 5: K2, SM, YO, K1, purl to marker, YO, SM, P1, SM, YO, purl to 1 st before marker, K1, YO, SM, K2.

Row 7: K2, SM, YO, K4, *K1, YO, K2, ssk, K2tog, K2, YO; rep from * to 4 sts before marker, K4, YO, SM, K1, SM, YO, K4, **YO, K2, ssk, K2tog, K2, YO, K1; rep from ** to 4 sts before marker, K4, YO, SM, K2.

Row 9: K2, YO, K5, *YO, K2, ssk, K2tog, K2, YO, K1; rep from * to 5 sts before marker, K5, YO, SM, K1, SM, YO, K5, **K1, YO, K2, ssk, K2tog, K2, YO; rep from ** to 5 sts before marker, K5, YO, SM, K2.

Rows 2, 4, and 6 (WS): K2, purl to last 2 sts, K2.

Row 3: K2, SM, YO, K5, YO, SM, K1, SM, YO, K5, YO, SM, K2—19 sts.

Row 5: K2, SM, YO, K7, YO, SM, K1, SM, YO, K7, YO, SM, K2—23 sts.

Row 7: K2, SM, YO, K9, YO, SM, K1, SM, YO, K9, YO, SM, K2—27 sts.

Row 8: K2, purl to last 2 sts, K2.

Work shawl chart 6 times. Work rows 1–11 of shawl chart once more.

STITCH COUNT FOR CHART REPEATS	
Rep 1 of chart	63 sts
Rep 2 of chart	99 sts
Rep 3 of chart	135 sts
Rep 4 of chart	171 sts
Rep 5 of chart	207 sts
Rep 6 of chart	243 sts
Rows 1–11 of chart	267 sts

» MAKE IT YOUR OWN!

It's easy to adjust the size of this shawl. Repeat the shawl chart to the desired length, ending with row 5, 11, or 17. So if you have more yarn left in your transitional or gradient yarn ball, you can keep going to use up every bit of the final color.

Row 11: Rep row 5.

Row 13: K2, SM, YO, K3, K2tog, K2, YO, *K1, YO, K2, ssk, K2tog, K2, YO; rep from * to 7 sts before marker, K1, YO, K2, ssk, K2, YO, SM, K1, SM, YO, K2, K2tog, K2, YO, K1, **YO, K2, ssk, K2tog, K2, YO, K1; rep from ** to 7 sts before marker, YO, K2, ssk, K3, YO, SM, K2.

Row 15: K2, SM, YO, K3, K2tog, K2, YO, K1, *YO, K2, ssk, K2tog, K2, YO, K1; rep from * to 8 sts before marker, YO, K2, ssk, K4, YO, SM, K1, SM, YO, K4, K2tog, K2, YO, **K1, YO, K2, ssk, K2tog, K2, YO; rep from ** to 8 sts before marker, K1, YO, K2, ssk, K3, YO, SM, K2.

Row 17: Rep row 5.

Row 18: K2, purl to last 2 sts, K2.

Rep rows 1–18 for patt.

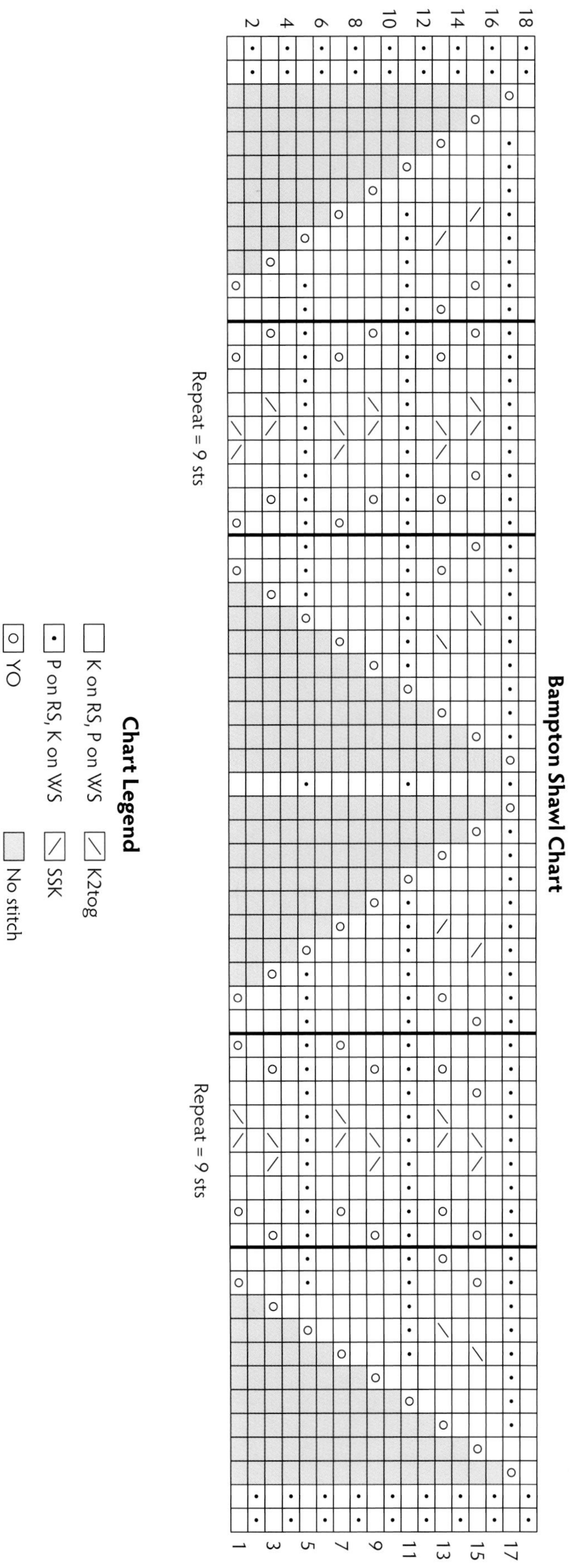

Chart Legend

☐	K on RS, P on WS
•	P on RS, K on WS
○	YO
╲	K2tog
╱	SSK
▨	No stitch

Bampton Shawl Chart

Repeat = 9 sts

POMELO TRIO

In the Pomelo Trio, mini bobbles and slipped stitches create the fun. The scarf, cowlette, and cowl each use two colors of yarn to build texture and interest. Try making one of the projects with two solid-color yarns, as shown above, or pair a variegated yarn in your slipped-stitch rows with a solid yarn to make something truly unique.

Pomelo Cowlette

DESIGNED AND KNIT BY THE AUTHOR

Like the Bampton Cowlette (page 51), this cowlette is worked by knitting a triangle shawl and then joining it in the round to transform it into a cowl. The stitch pattern differs slightly from the other pieces in this set; the bobble rows are worked progressively closer to each other as you work to the end of the piece.

Featured Yarns

Hawthorne Fingering from Knit Picks (80% superwash fine highland wool, 20% nylon; 100 g; 357 yds) in colors Poseidon (A: 1 skein) and Turkish Delight (B: 1 skein)

SKILL LEVEL: Intermediate

FINISHED MEASUREMENTS:
30" neck circumference; 18" long in front, and 7" long in back

MATERIALS

Yarn A 325 yards of fingering-weight yarn

Yarn B 150 yards of fingering-weight yarn

US size 4 (3.5 mm) circular needle, 24" cable, or size required for gauge

3 stitch markers

Tapestry needle

Blocking supplies

GAUGE

20 sts and 28 rows = 4" in St st

PATTERN NOTES

On the first slipped-stitch round, the stitch count increases to make the mini bobble. The stitch count returns back to the original count on the second slipped-stitch round.

Stunning Stitches

» The rows of mini bobbles emphasize the graceful triangle shape of the cowlette. The center back join keeps the cowlette from slipping off your shoulders.

INSTRUCTIONS

With A, work garter-tab CO (page 92) as follows: CO 3 sts. Knit 6 rows. Turn work 90° and pick up 3 sts along edge. Turn work 90° and pick up 3 sts from CO edge (9 sts total).

Stockinette Section (In rows)

Set-up row (WS): K3, YO, K1, PM, P1, PM, K1, YO, K3—11 sts.

Row 1 (RS): K2, YO, knit to marker, YO, SM, K1, SM, YO, knit to last 2 sts, YO, K2—15 sts.

Row 2 (WS): K3, YO, K1, purl to last 4 sts, K1, YO, K3.

Work rows 1 and 2 another 30 times (31 times total; 197 sts).

Rep row 1 once more—201 sts.

Do not turn work. You'll now be working in the round. Join rnd, being careful not to twist. PM to mark beg of rnd.

Lace Section (In the Round)

Set-up rnd: With A, knit all sts.

Rnd 1: With B, *(K1, YO, K1) in next st, sl 1 wyib; rep from * to last 3 sts, (K1, YO, K1) in next st, K2.

Rnd 2: With B, K2, *P3tog, sl 1 wyif; rep from * to last 5 sts, P3tog, K2.

Rnd 3: With A, K2, YO, knit to marker, YO, SM, K1, SM, YO, knit to last 2 sts, YO, K2 (205 sts).

Rnd 4: With A, knit all sts.

Rnds 5–12: Work rnds 3 and 4 another 4 times (221 sts).

Rnd 13: Rep rnd 1.

Rnd 14: Rep rnd 2.

Rnds 15–24: Work rnds 3 and 4 another 5 times (241 sts).

Rnd 25: Rep rnd 1.

Rnd 26: Rep rnd 2.

Rnds 27–32: Work rnds 3 and 4 another 3 times (253 sts).

Rnd 33: Rep rnd 1.

Rnd 34: Rep rnd 2.

Rnds 35–40: Work rnds 3 and 4 another 3 times (265 sts).

Rnd 41: Rep rnd 1.

Rnd 42: Rep rnd 2.

Rnds 43 and 44: Rep rnds 3 and 4 (269 sts).

Rnds 45–48: Rep rnds 41–44 (273 sts).

Rnd 49: Rep rnd 1.

Rnd 50: Rep rnd 2.

FINISHING

With A, BO loosely kw (page 92). Block cowlette to finished measurements given at beg of patt. With tapestry needle, weave in ends.

Stunning Stitches

Pomelo Cowl

DESIGNED AND KNIT BY THE AUTHOR

Quick, fun, and *cozy* are the perfect words to describe a piece that you'll want to wear all winter. If you knit the small size as I did here, you can finish your own Pomelo Cowl in just a few hours!

Featured Yarns

Preciosa Tonal from Knit Picks (100% merino wool; 100 g; 273 yds) in colors Crest (A: 1 [2] skein) and Pokeberry (B: 1 [2] skein)

SKILL LEVEL: Intermediate

SIZE: Cowl (Infinity Scarf)

FINISHED CIRCUMFERENCE: 25 (50)" slightly stretched

FINISHED LENGTH: 12"

MATERIALS

Yarn A 250 yards of worsted-weight yarn

Yarn B 150 yards of worsted-weight yarn

US size 8 (5.0 mm) circular needle, 16 (32)" cable, or size required for gauge
1 stitch marker
Tapestry needle
Blocking supplies

GAUGE

16 sts and 24 rows = 4" in St st in the round

Gauge is not critical in this patt, but a different gauge will affect yardage and size of cowl.

PATTERN NOTES

Pattern is written for cowl size with infinity scarf size in parentheses. If only one instruction is given, it should be worked for both sizes. Cowl size is shown.

On rounds 5 and 11, the stitch count increases to make the mini bobbles. The stitch count goes back down to 100 (200) stitches on rounds 6 and 12.

» Combining slipped stitches with small bobbles adds texture and contrast to an otherwise simple cowl.

» MAKE IT YOUR OWN!

As long as you cast on a multiple of two stitches, you can create whatever size cowl you want. Because this pattern is so easy to adjust, it's perfect for experimenting with different weights of yarn. Remember, adjusting the size will affect the amount of yarn you'll need.

When ending round 6, color B will be at the front of the work. Move this yarn to the back before starting round 7 with color A.

INSTRUCTIONS

With A, CO 100 (200) sts. Join rnd being careful not to twist. PM to mark beg of rnd.

Purl 1 rnd. Knit 1 rnd. Purl 1 rnd.

Rnds 1–4: With A, knit all sts.

Rnd 5: With B, *(K1, YO, K1) in next st, sl 1 wyib; rep from * to end.

Rnd 6: With B, *P3tog, sl 1 wyif; rep from * to end.

Rnds 7–10: With A, knit all sts.

Rnd 11: With B, *sl 1 wyib, (K1, YO, K1) in next st; rep from * to end.

Rnd 12: With B, *sl 1 wyif, P3tog; rep from * to end.

Work rnds 1–12 another 5 times. Rep rnds 1–10 once more. Cut B, yarn A will be used for remainder of cowl.

With A, purl 1 rnd. Knit 1 rnd. Purl 1 rnd.

FINISHING

BO loosely kw (page 92). Block cowl to finished measurements given at beg of patt. With tapestry needle, weave in ends.

Pomelo Scarf

DESIGNED BY THE AUTHOR AND KNIT BY JENNI LESNIAK

Completely addicting to knit, these bobbles are a fun way to show off your favorite color combination. The stitch count can easily be altered to make a different size scarf if desired. The length I've designed is long enough to wrap around your neck for warmth without being too bulky.

Featured Yarns

Gloss DK from Knit Picks (70% merino wool, 30% silk; 50 g; 123 yds) in colors Aegean (A: 3 balls) and Sweetheart (B: 2 balls)

SKILL LEVEL: Intermediate

FINISHED MEASUREMENTS: 7" × 72"

MATERIALS

Yarn A 350 yards of DK-weight yarn

Yarn B 200 yards of DK-weight yarn

US size 6 (4.0 mm) knitting needles, or size required for gauge

Tapestry needle

Blocking supplies

GAUGE

22 sts and 28 rows = 4" in St st

Gauge is not critical in this patt, but a different gauge will affect yardage and size of scarf.

PATTERN NOTES

On rows 5 and 11, the stitch count increases to make the mini bobbles. The stitch count goes back down to 37 stitches on rows 6 and 12.

Stunning Stitches

INSTRUCTIONS

With A, CO 37 sts. Knit 1 row on WS.

Row 1 (RS): With A, knit all sts.

Row 2 (WS): K2, purl to last 2 sts, K2.

Row 3: Knit all sts.

Row 4: K2, purl to last 2 sts, K2.

Row 5: With B, K2, *(K1, YO, K1) in next st, sl 1 wyib; rep from * to last 3 sts, (K1, YO, K1) in next st, K2.

Row 6: With B, K2, *K3tog tbl, sl 1 wyib; rep from * to last 3 sts, K3tog tbl, K2.

Rows 7–10: With A, rep rows 1–4.

Row 11: With B, K2, *sl 1 wyib, (K1, YO, K1) in next st; rep from * to last 3 sts, sl 1 wyib, K2.

Row 12: With B, K2, *sl 1 wyib, K3tog tbl; rep from * to last 3 sts, sl 1 wyib, K2.

Rep rows 1–12 until scarf measures approx 68", ending with row 9. With A, knit 1 row on WS.

FINISHING

BO loosely kw (page 92) on RS. Block scarf to finished measurements given at beg of patt. With tapestry needle, weave in ends.

» Offsetting the bobbles on the scarf creates extra interest. For even more flair, use a variegated yarn for color B.

» MAKE IT YOUR OWN!

It's easy to change the width of this scarf. Cast on any multiple of two and then add five stitches to get the perfect scarf for you. Don't forget—changing your stitch count will affect the amount of yarn you'll need.

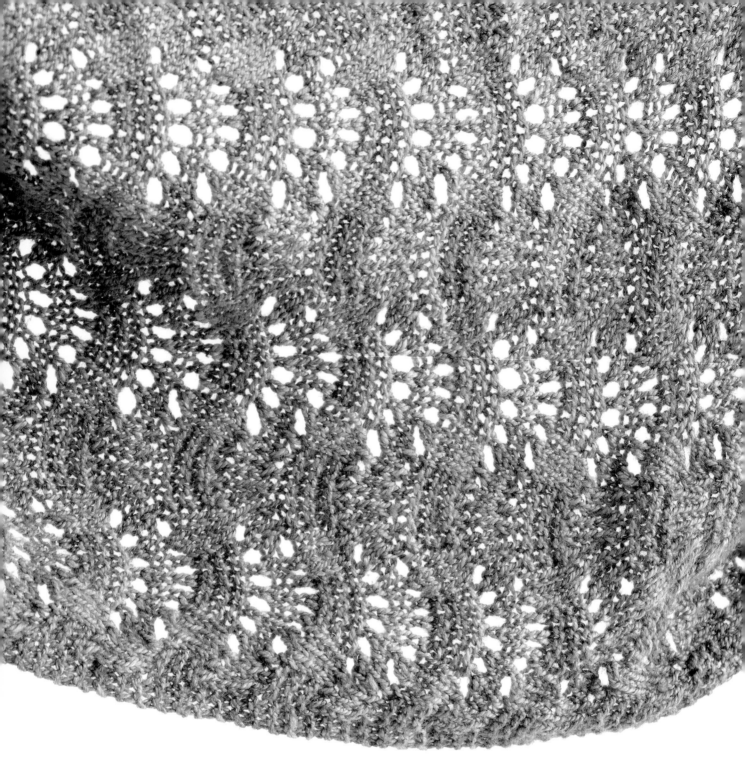

VIOLETEAR TRIO

As I love pairing garter stitch with beautiful lace patterns, it's no surprise
that I was drawn to this stunning feather-and-fan stitch pattern. A gorgeous
and luxurious yarn highlights the oscillating lace in each of the patterns in
the Violetear Trio: a shawl, an infinity scarf, and a seamed cowl.

Violetear Shawl

DESIGNED AND KNIT BY THE AUTHOR

I know that many knitters love bottom-up short-row shawls just as much as I do. I've designed many of them over the years, but this one is my favorite. The way the feather-and-fan lace flows into the garter-stitch body of the shawl makes me happy. I hope it makes you happy too!

Featured Yarn

2 skeins of CashLuxe Fine from Sweet Georgia Yarns (70% superwash merino wool, 20% cashmere, 10% nylon; 115 g; 400 yds) in color Laurel

SKILL LEVEL: Intermediate

FINISHED MEASUREMENTS: 62" across from point to point and 12" long from neck to bottom edge at center

MATERIALS

600 yards of fingering-weight yarn
US size 5 (3.75 mm) circular needle, 24" cable, or size required for gauge
Tapestry needle
Blocking supplies

GAUGE

16 sts and 32 rows = 4" in garter st

Gauge is not critical in this patt, but a different gauge will affect yardage and size of shawl.

Pattern Notes

Charts are on page 72. If you prefer to follow written instructions for charted material, see "Written Instructions for Charts" on page 71.

Stunning Stitches

» Small garter-stitch details within the feather-and-fan lace make this the ideal pattern to use in a shawl with a garter-stitch body.

INSTRUCTIONS

CO 363 sts.

Foundation row (WS): Knit. Work chart A 3 times—36 rows. Work chart B once—279 sts.

Work short rows as follows:

Row 1 (RS): K144, turn work—135 sts unworked.

Row 2 (WS): K9, turn work—135 sts unworked.

Row 3: K8, ssk, K4, turn work —130 sts unworked; 278 sts total.

Row 4: K8, K2tog, K4, turn work—130 sts unworked; 277 sts total.

Row 5: Knit to 1 st before gap (1 st before previous turning point), ssk, K4, turn work.

Row 6: Knit to 1 st before gap (1 st before previous turning point), K2tog, K4, turn work.

Work rows 5 and 6 another 25 times. All sts have been worked—225 sts.

FINISHING

BO loosely kw (page 92) on RS. Block shawl to finished measurements given at beg of patt. With tapestry needle, weave in ends.

WRITTEN INSTRUCTIONS FOR CHARTS

If you prefer to follow row-by-row written instructions rather than a chart, use the instructions below.

Chart A

Row 1 (RS): K3, *ssk 3 times, (YO, K1) 5 times, YO, K2tog 3 times; rep from * to last 3 sts, K3.

Row 2 and all even-numbered rows (WS): K3, purl to last 3 sts, K3.

Row 3: Knit all sts.

Row 5: Rep row 1.

Rows 7, 9 and 11: K3, *P3, K3, P5, K3, P3; rep from * to last 3 sts, K3.

Row 12: K3, purl to last 3 sts, K3.

Rep rows 1–12 for patt.

Chart B

Row 1 (RS): K3, *ssk 3 times, (YO, K1) 5 times, YO, K2tog 3 times; rep from * to last 3 sts, K3.

Rows 2, 4, 6, 8, 10, 12, 14, and 16 (WS): K3, purl to last 3 sts, K3.

Row 3: Knit all sts.

Row 5: Rep row 1.

Rows 7, 9 and 11: K3, *P3, K3, P5, K3, P3; rep from * to last 3 sts, K3.

Row 13: K3, *ssk 3 times, (K1, YO) 4 times, K1, K2tog 3 times; rep from * to last 3 sts, K3.

Row 15: Knit all sts.

Row 17: K3, *ssk 3 times, K2, YO, K1, YO, K2, K2tog 3 times; rep from * to last 3 sts, K3.

Row 18: Knit all sts.

Violetear Chart A

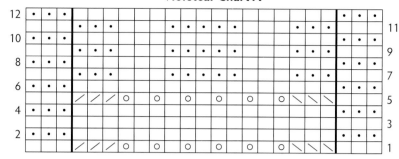

Repeat = 17 sts

Violetear Chart B

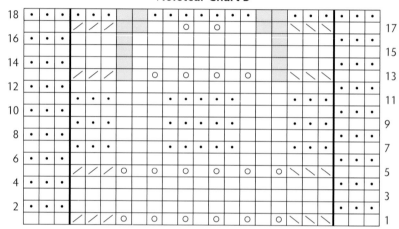

Repeat = 17 sts

Chart Legend

□ K on RS, P on WS	╱ K2tog	
• P on RS, K on WS	╲ SSK	
○ YO	▨ No stitch	

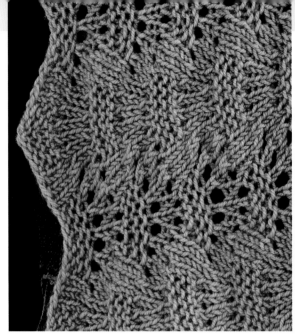

Violetear Infinity Scarf

DESIGNED BY THE AUTHOR AND KNIT BY JENNI LESNIAK

This infinity scarf is the perfect piece for a cool evening. The openness of the lovely lace pattern makes it an ideal, lightweight accessory to wear in spring or fall. Delicate and fancy, it's great for a "date night."

Featured Yarn

1 (2) skein of Superwash Sport from Sweet Georgia Yarns (100% superwash merino wool; 100 g; 328 yds) in color Hush

SKILL LEVEL: Intermediate

SIZE: Cowl (Infinity Scarf)

FINISHED CIRCUMFERENCE: 24 (48)", slightly stretched

FINISHED LENGTH: 13"

MATERIALS

320 (640) yards of sport-weight yarn (2)
US size 6 (4.00 mm) circular needle, 16 (32)" cable, or size required for gauge

1 stitch marker
Tapestry needle
Blocking supplies

GAUGE

24 sts and 28 rows = 4" in St st in the round

Gauge is not critical in this patt, but a different gauge will affect yardage and size of cowl.

PATTERN NOTES

Pattern is written for cowl size with infinity scarf size in parentheses. If only one instruction is given, it should be worked for both sizes. Infinity scarf size is shown.

Chart is on page 75. If you prefer to follow written instructions for the charted material, see "Written Instructions for Chart" on page 75.

74   *Stunning Stitches*

Instructions

CO 136 (272) sts. Join rnd, being careful not to twist. PM to mark beg of rnd.

Work chart 6 times (72 rnds). Work rnds 1–5 of chart once more.

FINISHING

BO loosely kw (page 92). Block cowl to finished measurements given at beg of patt. With tapestry needle, weave in ends.

WRITTEN INSTRUCTIONS FOR CHART

If you prefer to follow written instructions rather than a chart, use the instructions below.

Rnd 1: *P3, K3, P5, K3, P3 ; rep from * to end of rnd.

Rnd 2: Knit all sts.

Rnds 3–6: Rep rnds 1 and 2 twice.

Rnd 7: *Ssk 3 times, (YO, K1) 5 times, YO, K2tog 3 times; rep from * to end of rnd.

Rnds 8–10: Knit all sts.

Rnd 11: Rep rnd 7.

Rnd 12: Knit all sts.

Rep rnds 1–12 for patt.

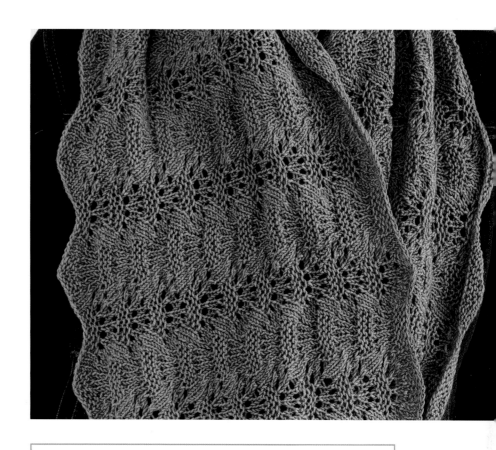

> **» MAKE IT YOUR OWN!**
>
> Cast on any multiple of 17 stitches to create whatever size cowl you want. Remember, adjusting the size will affect the amount of yarn you'll need.

Violetear Infinity Scarf Chart

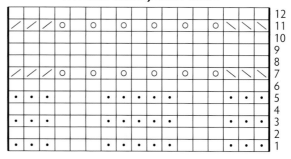

Repeat = 17 sts

Chart Legend

☐	K	⁄	K2tog
•	P	＼	SSK
⊙	YO		

Stunning Stitches

Violetear Cowl

DESIGNED BY THE AUTHOR AND KNIT BY JENNI LESNIAK

Show off the feather-and-fan stitch pattern in a garment that's a clever twist on the traditional cowl. The piece is worked flat, and a partial seam is added at the end to give you a variety of ways to wear it.

Yarn Used for Featured Cowl

3 skeins of Silk Crush from Sweet Georgia Yarns (50% superwash merino wool, 50% silk; 115 g; 375 yds) in color Mist

---

SKILL LEVEL: Intermediate

FINISHED MEASUREMENTS:
60" × 16", before seaming

MATERIALS

850 yards of fingering-weight yarn
US size 5 (3.75 mm) knitting needles, or size required for gauge
Tapestry needle
Blocking supplies

GAUGE

20 sts and 28 rows = 4" in St st

Gauge is not critical in this patt, but a different gauge will affect yardage and size of scarf.

PATTERN NOTES

Chart is on page 78. If you prefer to follow written instructions for the charted material, see "Written Instructions for Chart" on page 78.

INSTRUCTIONS

CO 91 sts.

Foundation row (WS): Knit.

Work chart until piece measures approx 54" from CO edge, ending with row 5. Knit 1 row on WS.

FINISHING

BO loosely kw (page 92). Block piece to finished measurements given at beg of patt. With tapestry needle, weave in ends. Fold in half lengthwise (lining up CO and

BO edges). Starting at CO/BO edge, whipstitch 6" along one lengthwise edge. Leave remainder of edge unsewn.

WRITTEN INSTRUCTIONS FOR CHART

If you prefer to follow row-by-row written instructions rather than a chart, use the instructions below.

Row 1 (RS): K3, *ssk 3 times, (YO, K1) 5 times, YO, K2tog 3 times; rep from * to last 3 sts, K3.

Row 2 and all even-numbered rows (WS): K3, purl to last 3 sts, K3.

Row 3: Knit all sts.

Row 5: Rep row 1.

Row 7: K3, *P3, K3, P5, K3, P3; rep from * to last 3 sts, K3.

Row 9: Rep row 7.

Row 11: Rep row 7.

Row 12: K3, purl to last 3 sts, K3.

Rep rows 1–12 for patt.

» By working the piece flat and then seaming the ends together, you create an accessory that can be worn in a variety of interesting ways.

Violetear Cowl Chart

Repeat = 17 sts

Chart Legend

☐	K on RS, P on WS	╱	K2tog
•	P on RS, K on WS	╲	SSK
○	YO		

Stunning Stitches

POTRERO HILL TRIO

Seed stitch and lace are paired together in this set to zig and zag across your accessories. The lace reminds me of a winding road with lots of hairpin turns. A smooth and springy hand-dyed yarn showcases the texture and airiness of these projects.

Stunning Stitches

Potrero Hill Shawl

DESIGNED BY AUTHOR AND KNIT BY MELISSA RUSK

This sophisticated semicircular shawl is a perfect showcase for seed stitch and lace. Using traditional pi-shawl math, you can make this shawl as big as you want. Notes on how to enlarge it are included in the pattern.

Featured Yarn

3 skeins of Breathless DK from Shalimar Yarns (75% superwash merino, 15% cashmere; 10% silk; 270 yds) in color Bing

---

SKILL LEVEL: Intermediate

FINISHED MEASUREMENTS:
60" × 24"

MATERIALS

740 yards of DK-weight yarn
US size 6 (4.0 mm) circular
   needle, 32" cable or longer,
   or size required for gauge
Tapestry needle
Blocking supplies

GAUGE

18 sts and 24 rows = 4" in St st

Gauge is not critical in this patt, but a different gauge will affect yardage and size of shawl.

PATTERN NOTES

Charts are on page 84. If you prefer to follow written instructions for the charted material, see "Written Instructions for Charts" on page 82.

INSTRUCTIONS

Work garter-tab CO (page 92) as follows: CO 2 sts. Knit 20 rows. Turn work 90° and pick up 10 sts along the edge. Turn work 90° and pick up 2 sts from CO edge— 14 sts total.

Set-up row (WS): Knit all sts.

Row 1 (RS): K2, (YO, K1) to last 2 sts, K2 (24 sts).

Row 2: K2, purl to last 2 sts, K2.

Row 3: Knit all sts.

Row 4: Rep row 2.

Body of Shawl

Inc Row (RS): K2, (YO, K1) to last 2 sts, K2—44 sts.

Row 2 (WS): K2, purl to last 2 sts, K2.

Row 3: Knit all sts.

Work rows 2 and 3 another 3 times. Rep row 2 once more.

Work inc row—84 sts.

Next row: Rep row 2.

Work chart A once (14 rows).

Work inc row—164 sts.

Next row: Rep row 2.

Work chart B once (28 rows).

Work inc row—324 sts.

Next row: Rep row 2.

Work chart B twice (56 rows).

Work rows 1–14 of chart B once more.

FINISHING

BO loosely kw (page 92) on RS. Block shawl to finished measurements given at beg of patt. With tapestry needle, weave in ends.

> **» MAKE IT YOUR OWN!**
>
> For an even larger shawl, work the increase row again (644 stitches) and continue working chart B to the desired length, ending with row 14 or 28. Remember, adjusting the size will affect the amount of yarn you'll need.

WRITTEN INSTRUCTIONS FOR CHARTS

If you prefer to follow row-by-row written instructions rather than a chart, use the instructions below.

Chart A

Row 1 (RS): K2, *K6, (YO, K2tog) twice; rep from * to last 2 sts, K2.

Row 2 (WS): K2, *K1, P9; rep from * to last 2 sts, K2.

Row 3: K2, *K5, (YO, K2tog) twice, K1; rep from * to last 2 sts, K2.

Row 4: Rep row 2.

Row 5: K2, *K4, (YO, K2tog) twice, P1, K1; rep from * to last 2 sts, K2.

Row 6: K2, *K1, P1, K1, P7; rep from * to last 2 sts, K2.

Row 7: K2, *K3, (YO, K2tog) twice, K1, P1, K1; rep from * to last 2 sts, K2.

Row 8: Rep row 6.

Row 9: K2, *K2, (YO, K2tog) twice, (P1, K1) twice; rep from * to last 2 sts, K2.

Row 10: K2, *(K1, P1) twice, K1, P5; rep from * to last 2 sts, K2.

Row 11: K2, *K1 (YO, K2tog) twice, (K1, P1) twice, K1; rep from * to last 2 sts, K2.

Row 12: Rep row 10.

Row 13: K2, *(YO, K2tog) twice, (P1, K1) 3 times; rep from * to last 2 sts, K2.

Row 14: Rep row 10.

Rep rows 1–14 for patt.

Chart B

Row 1 (RS): K2, *(ssk, YO) twice, K6; rep from * to last 2 sts, K2.

Row 2 (WS): K2, *P9, K1; rep from * to last 2 sts, K2.

Row 3: K2, *K1, (ssk, YO) twice, K5; rep from * to last 2 sts, K2.

Row 4: Rep row 2.

Row 5: K2, *K1, P1, (ssk, YO) twice, K4; rep from * to last 2 sts, K2.

Row 6: K2, *P7, K1, P1, K1; rep from * to last 2 sts, K2.

Row 7: K2, *K1 P1, K1, (ssk, YO) twice, K3; rep from * to last 2 sts, K2.

Row 8: Rep row 6.

Row 9: K2, *(K1 P1) twice, (ssk, YO) twice, K2; rep from * to last 2 sts, K2.

Row 10: K2, *P5, (K1, P1) twice, K1; rep from * to last 2 sts, K2.

Row 11: K2, *(K1, P1) twice, K1, (ssk, YO) twice, K1; rep from * to last 2 sts, K2.

Row 12: Rep row 10.

Row 13: K2, *(K1, P1) 3 times, (ssk, YO) twice; rep from * to last 2 sts, K2.

Row 14: Rep row 10.

Row 15: K2, *K6, (YO, K2tog) twice; rep from * to last 2 sts, K2.

Row 16: K2, *K1, P9; rep from * to last 2 sts, K2.

Row 17: K2, *K5, (YO, K2tog) twice, K1; rep from * to last 2 sts, K2.

Row 18: Rep row 16.

Row 19: K2, *K4, (YO, K2tog) twice, P1, K1; rep from * to last 2 sts, K2.

Row 20: K2, *K1, P1, K1, P7; rep from * to last 2 sts, K2.

Row 21: K2, *K3, (YO, K2tog) twice, K1, P1, K1; rep from * to last 2 sts, K2.

Row 22: Rep row 20.

Row 23: K2, *K2, (YO, K2tog) twice, (P1, K1) twice; rep from * to last 2 sts, K2.

Row 24: K2, *(K1, P1) twice, K1, P5; rep from * to last 2 sts, K2.

Row 25: K2, *K1 (YO, K2tog) twice, (K1, P1) twice, K1; rep from * to last 2 sts, K2.

Row 26: Rep row 24.

Row 27: K2, *(YO, K2tog) twice, (P1, K1) 3 times; rep from * to last 2 sts, K2.

Row 28: Rep row 24.

Rep rows 1–28 for patt.

Potrero Hill Shawl Chart A

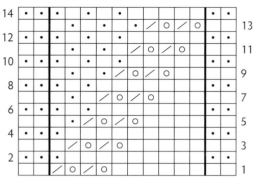

Repeat = 10 sts

Potrero Hill Shawl Chart B

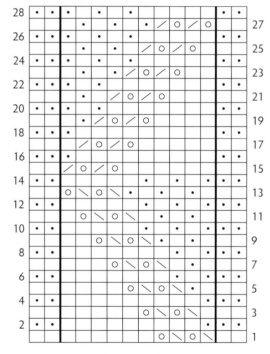

Repeat = 10 sts

Chart Legend

☐ K on RS, P on WS	╱ K2tog
⊡ P on RS, K on WS	╲ SSK
⊙ YO	

Potrero Hill Cowl

DESIGNED BY THE AUTHOR AND KNIT BY MELISSA RUSK

This quick cowl is an excellent project if you're new to seed stitch. You'll have it mastered in no time! The zigzag pattern dances gracefully down the length of the cowl for lots of texture and interest.

Featured Yarn

1 (2) skein of Aerie from Shalimar Yarns (70% superwash merino, 20% kid mohair, 10% silk; 420 yds) in color Primula

SKILL LEVEL: Intermediate

SIZE: Cowl (Infinity Scarf)

FINISHED CIRCUMFERENCE:
24 (48)", slightly stretched

FINISHED LENGTH: 10"

MATERIALS

250 (500) yards of fingering-
weight yarn (1)
US size 5 (3.75 mm) circular
needle, 16 (32)" cable, or size
required for gauge

1 stitch marker
Tapestry needle
Blocking supplies

GAUGE

22 sts and 32 rows = 4" in St st
in the round

Gauge is not critical in this patt,
but a different gauge will affect
yardage and size of cowl.

PATTERN NOTES

Pattern is written for cowl size
with infinity scarf size in
parentheses. If only one
instruction is given, it should
be worked for both sizes. Cowl
sizeis shown.

Cowl chart is on page 87. If
you prefer to follow written
instructions for the charted
material, see "Written
Instructions for Chart" on
page 87.

Stunning Stitches

INSTRUCTIONS

CO 130 (260) sts. Join rnd, being careful not to twist. PM to mark beg of rnd.

Ribbing rnd: *K4, P2, K2, P2; rep from * to end of rnd.

Rep ribbing rnd 5 times (6 rnds total).

Work chart 3 times (84 rnds).

Work ribbing rnd for 6 rnds.

FINISHING

BO all sts loosely in patt. Block cowl to finished measurements given at beg of patt. With tapestry needle, weave in ends.

Written Instructions for Chart

If you prefer to follow written instructions rather than a chart, use the instructions below.

Rnd 1: *(Ssk, YO) twice, K6; rep from * to end of rnd.

Rnd 2: *P1, K9; rep from * to end of rnd.

Rnd 3: *K1, (ssk, YO) twice, K5; rep from * to end of rnd.

Rnd 4: Rep rnd 2.

Rnd 5: *K1, P1, (ssk, YO) twice, K4; rep from * to end of rnd.

Rnd 6: *P1, K1, P1, K7; rep from * to end of rnd.

Rnd 7: *K1, P1, K1, (ssk, YO) twice, K3; rep from * to end of rnd.

Rnd 8: Rep rnd 6.

Rnd 9: *(K1, P1) twice, (ssk, YO) twice, K2; rep from * to end of rnd.

Rnd 10: *(P1, K1) twice, P1, K5; rep from * to end of rnd.

Rnd 11: *(K1, P1) twice, K1, (ssk, YO) twice, K1; rep from * to end of rnd.

Rnd 12: Rep rnd 10.

Rnd 13: *(K1, P1) 3 times, (ssk, YO) twice; rep from * to end of rnd.

Rnd 14: Rep rnd 10.

Rnd 15: *K6, (YO, K2tog) twice; rep from * to end of rnd.

Rnd 16: *K9, P1; rep from * to end of rnd.

Rnd 17: *K5, (YO, K2tog) twice, K1; rep from * to end of rnd.

Rnd 18: Rep rnd 16.

Rnd 19: *K4, (YO, K2tog) twice, P1, K1; rep from * to end of rnd.

Rnd 20: *K7, P1, K1, P1; rep from * to end of rnd.

Rnd 21: *K3, (YO, K2tog) twice, K1, P1, K1; rep from * to end of rnd.

Rnd 22: Rep rnd 20.

Rnd 23: *K2, (YO, K2tog) twice, (P1, K1) twice; rep from * to end of rnd.

Rnd 24: *K5, (P1, K1) twice, P1; rep from * to end of rnd.

Rnd 25: *K1, (YO, K2tog) twice, (K1, P1) twice, K1; rep from * to end of rnd.

Rnd 26: Rep rnd 24.

Rnd 27: *(YO, K2tog) twice, (P1, K1) 3 times; rep from * to end of rnd.

Rnd 28: Rep rnd 24.

Rep rnds 1–28 for patt.

> **» MAKE IT YOUR OWN!**
>
> Cast on any multiple of 10 stitches to create whatever size cowl you want. Remember, adjusting the size will affect the amount of yarn you'll need.

Potrero Hill Cowl Chart

										Row
•		•		•						28
	•		•		•	∕	o	∕	o	27
•		•		•						26
	•		•		∕	o	∕	o		25
•		•		•						24
	•		•	∕	o	∕	o			23
•		•								22
	•		∕	o	∕	o				21
•		•								20
	•	∕	o	∕	o					19
•										18
	∕	o	∕	o						17
•										16
∕	o	∕	o							15
					•		•		•	14
o	\	o	\	•		•		•		13
					•		•		•	12
	o	\	o	\		•		•		11
					•		•		•	10
		o	\	o	\	•		•		9
							•		•	8
			o	\	o	\		•		7
							•		•	6
				o	\	o	\	•		5
									•	4
					o	\	o	\		3
									•	2
						o	\	o	\	1

Repeat = 10 sts

Chart Legend

Symbol	Meaning	Symbol	Meaning
☐	K	∕	K2tog
•	P	\	SSK
o	YO		

Stunning Stitches

Potrero Hill Stole

DESIGNED BY THE AUTHOR AND KNIT BY JENNI LESNIAK

For this stunning showpiece stole, use a smooth yarn that shows off the stitch pattern.
Like all the other scarves and stoles in this book, you can make this stole any size you like.

Yarn Used for Featured Stole

2 skeins of Breathless from Shalimar Yarns (75% superwash merino, 15% cashmere, 10% silk; 420 yds) in color Black Truffle

---

SKILL LEVEL: Intermediate

FINISHED MEASUREMENTS:
68" × 14"

MATERIALS

820 yards of fingering-weight yarn
US size 5 (3.75 mm) knitting needles or size required for gauge
Tapestry needle
Blocking supplies

GAUGE

20 sts and 32 rows = 4" in St st

Gauge is not critical in this patt, but a different gauge will affect yardage and size of scarf.

PATTERN NOTES

Chart is on page 91. If you prefer to follow written instructions for the charted material, see "Written Instructions for Chart" on page 90.

INSTRUCTIONS

CO 64 sts. Knit 1 row on WS. Work chart until piece measures approx 64" from CO edge, ending with row 27. Knit 1 row on WS.

FINISHING

BO loosely kw (page 92) on WS. Block stole to finished measurements given at beg of patt. With tapestry needle, weave in ends.

» The generous dimensions of the stole combined with the open stitch pattern make it cozy yet lightweight.

> ### » MAKE IT YOUR OWN!
>
> If you'd like to make a smaller scarf, cast on 34 stitches. As long as you cast on a multiple of 10 plus 4 stitches, the scarf can be any size you like.

Written Instructions for Chart

If you prefer to follow row-by-row written instructions rather than a chart, use the instructions below.

Row 1 (RS): K2, *(ssk, YO) twice, K6; rep from * to last 2 sts, K2.

Row 2 (WS): K2, *P9, K1; rep from * to last 2 sts, K2.

Row 3: K2, *K1, (ssk, YO) twice, K5; rep from * to last 2 sts, K2.

Row 4: Rep row 2.

Row 5: K2, *K1, P1, (ssk, YO) twice, K4; rep from * to last 2 sts, K2.

Row 6: K2, *P7, K1, P1, K1; rep from * to last 2 sts, K2.

Row 7: K2, *K1 P1, K1, (ssk, YO) twice, K3; rep from * to last 2 sts, K2.

Row 8: Rep row 6.

Row 9: K2, *(K1 P1) twice, (ssk, YO) twice, K2; rep from * to last 2 sts, K2.

Row 10: K2, *P5, (K1, P1) twice, K1; rep from * to last 2 sts, K2.

Row 11: K2, *(K1, P1) twice, K1, (ssk, YO) twice, K1; rep from * to last 2 sts, K2.

Row 12: Rep row 10.

Row 13: K2, *(K1, P1) 3 times, (ssk, YO) twice; rep from * to last 2 sts, K2.

Row 14: Rep row 10.

Row 15: K2, *K6, (YO, K2tog) twice; rep from * to last 2 sts, K2.

Row 16: K2, *K1, P9; rep from * to last 2 sts, K2.

Row 17: K2, *K5, (YO, K2tog) twice, K1; rep from * to last 2 sts, K2.

Row 18: Rep row 16.

Row 19: K2, *K4, (YO, K2tog) twice, P1, K1; rep from * to last 2 sts, K2.

Row 20: K2, *K1, P1, K1, P7; rep from * to last 2 sts, K2.

Row 21: K2, *K3, (YO, K2tog) twice, K1, P1, K1; rep from * to last 2 sts, K2.

Row 22: Rep row 20.

Row 23: K2, *K2, (YO, K2tog) twice, (P1, K1) twice; rep from * to last 2 sts, K2.

Row 24: K2, *(K1, P1) twice, K1, P5; rep from * to last 2 sts, K2.

Row 25: K2, *K1, (YO, K2tog) twice, (K1, P1) twice, K1; rep from * to last 2 sts, K2.

Row 26: Rep row 24.

Row 27: K2, *(YO, K2tog) twice, (P1, K1) 3 times; rep from * to last 2 sts, K2.

Row 28: Rep row 24.

Rep rows 1–28 for patt.

Potrero Hill Stole Chart

Repeat = 10 sts

Chart Legend

☐ K on RS, P on WS   ╱ K2tog

• P on RS, K on WS   ╲ SSK

○ YO

SPECIAL TECHNIQUES

The following techniques are used throughout the book and will help you successfully knit your projects.

GARTER-TAB CAST ON

Several projects in this book begin with a garter-tab cast on. This cast on is typically worked as follows.

1. Cast on three stitches and knit six rows.

2. Rotate work clockwise 90° and pick up three stitches evenly along the edge. Try to insert the needle into each of the three bumps on the edge of the tab.

3. Rotate work clockwise 90° and pick up three stitches evenly from the cast-on edge (nine stitches total). Turn your work and continue with row 1 of the pattern.

KNITWISE BIND OFF

For a shawl, the goal is to have a bind off that's stretchy so that when blocking, you can pull and form the edge any way you like. If you tend to bind off tightly, use a needle one or two sizes larger.

To work, knit the first two stitches together through the back loop. *Slip the stitch from the right needle to the left needle with the yarn in back and knit two together through the back loops; repeat from * until all stitches are bound off.

KITCHENER STITCH

Kitchener stitch is a great finishing technique to learn—by grafting two pieces of knitted fabric together, such as two halves of a scarf, you create a seamless piece, which gives your projects an extra-special finished touch. To work Kitchener stitch:

1. Arrange stitches on two needles, with the same number of stitches on each needle.

2. Thread a tapestry needle with the working yarn attached to the back needle.

3. Insert tapestry needle through the first stitch on the front needle as if to purl and leave on the needle.

4. Insert tapestry needle through the first stitch on the back needle as if to knit and leave on the needle.

5. Insert tapestry needle through the first front stitch as if to knit and slip stitch off the needle.

6. Then insert needle through the next stitch on the front needle as if to purl and leave on the needle.

7. Insert tapestry needle through the first stitch on the back needle as if to purl and slip stitch off the needle. Then insert needle through the next stitch on the back needle as if to knit and leave on the needle.

Repeat steps 5 and 6 until all sts have been worked.

USEFUL INFORMATION

Yarn-Weight Symbol and Category Name	[1] Super Fine	[2] Fine	[3] Light	[4] Medium	[5] Bulky	[6] Super Bulky
Types of Yarn in Category	Sock, Fingering, Baby	Sport, Baby	DK, Light Worsted	Worsted, Afghan, Aran	Chunky, Craft, Rug	Bulky, Roving
Knit Gauge Range* in Stockinette Stitch to 4"	27 to 32 sts	23 to 26 sts	21 to 24 sts	16 to 20 sts	12 to 15 sts	6 to 11 sts
Recommended Needle in US Size Range	1 to 3	3 to 5	5 to 7	7 to 9	9 to 11	11 and larger
Recommended Needle in Metric Size Range	2.25 to 3.25 mm	3.25 to 3.75 mm	3.75 to 4.5 mm	4.5 to 5.5 mm	5.5 to 8 mm	8 mm and larger

*These are guidelines only. The above reflect the most commonly used gauges and needles for specific yarn categories.

KNITTING NEEDLE SIZES

US Size	Size in Millimeters
1	2.25 mm
2	2.75 mm
3	3.25 mm
4	3.5 mm
5	3.75 mm
6	4 mm
7	4.5 mm
8	5 mm
9	5.5 mm
10	6 mm
10½	6.5 mm
11	8 mm
13	9 mm
15	10 mm
17	12.75 mm
19	15 mm
35	19 mm
50	25 mm

METRIC CONVERSION

Yards	=	meters	x	1.0936
Meters	=	yards	x	0.9144
Ounces	=	grams	x	0.0352
Grams	=	ounces	x	28.35

SKILL LEVELS

Easy: Projects using basic stitches, repetitive stitch patterns, and simple color changes; simple shaping and finishing.

Intermediate: Projects using a variety of stitches, such as basic cables and lace, simple intarsia, and techniques for double-pointed needles and knitting in the round; mid-level shaping and finishing.

Experienced: Projects using advanced techniques and stitches, such as short rows, Fair Isle, more intricate intarsia, cables, lace patterns, and numerous color changes.

ABBREVIATIONS AND GLOSSARY

[ ] Work instructions within brackets as many times as directed.

( ) Work instructions within parentheses in the place directed.

* Repeat instructions following the single asterisk as directed.

** Repeat instructions following the asterisks as directed.

" inch(es)

approx approximately

beg begin(ning)

BO bind off

ch(s) chain(s)

cn cable needle(s)

CO cast on

cont continue(ing)(s)

est established

inc(s) increase(ing)(s)

K knit

K1f&b knit into front and back of same stitch—1 stitch increased

K2tog knit 2 stitches together—1 stitch decreased

kw knitwise

LH left hand

mm millimeter(s)

oz ounce(s)

P purl

patt(s) pattern(s)

P2tog purl 2 stitches together—1 stitch decreased

P3tog purl 3 stitches together—2 stitches decreased

PM place marker

PU pick up and knit

pw purlwise

rem remain(ing)

rep(s) repeat(s)

RH right hand

rnd(s) round(s)

RS right side

sk2p slip 1 knitwise, knit 2 together, pass slipped stitch over the knit 2 together—2 stitches decreased

sl slip

sl st slip stitch(es)—slip stitches purlwise unless instructed otherwise

SM slip marker

ssk slip 2 stitches knitwise, 1 at a time, to right needle, then insert left needle from left to right into front loops and knit 2 stitches together—1 stitch decreased

st(s) stitch(es)

St st stockinette stitch(es)

tbl through back loop(s)

tog together

WS wrong side

wyib with yarn in back

wyif with yarn in front

YO(s) yarn over(s)

YARN SOURCES

Anzula Luxury Fibers
www.Anzula.com
Cloud
For Better or Worsted
Cricket

Stitch Sprouts
www.StitchSprouts.com
Yellowstone
Crater Lake

Done Roving Yarns
www.DoneRoving.com
Gradient DK Weight
Tapping Tootsees
Frolicking Feet Transitions

Lorna's Laces
www.LornasLaces.net
Shepherd Sport
Shepherd Bulky
Shepherd Worsted

Knit Picks
www.KnitPicks.com
Gloss DK
Hawthorne
Preciosa Tonal

Sweet Georgia Yarns
www.SweetGeorgiaYarns.com
CashLuxe Fine
Superwash Sport
Silk Crush

Shalimar Yarns
www.ShalimarYarns.com
Breathless DK
Aerie
Breathless

Yarn in the Box
www.YarnintheBox.com
Posh Panda

ACKNOWLEDGMENTS

I'm forever grateful to have the job that I have today. I love writing knitting patterns, and it's because of the tremendous amount of support from those around me that I get to be living the dream. Thank you to my sample knitters: Jenni Lesniak, Cathy Rusk, and Melissa Rusk. Not only do you do amazing work, you're incredible friends. Thank you also to the entire Martingale team. I'm thankful that I've found such an amazing group of people to work with and they enjoy crafting as much as I do.

Thank you to all the knitters who have read my blog, bought a pattern, joined one of my knit-alongs, or enjoyed the patterns in one of my previous books. You've given me the greatest gift—the ability to have this awesome job where I get to play with yarn all day. I hope I can continue to make patterns that you love to knit.

As always, thank you to my husband, Alex. You continue to be the most amazing support. I couldn't do this without you.

ABOUT THE AUTHOR

Jen has been knitting since 2004 and designing since 2008. Her designs have appeared in several magazines, including *Interweave Knits, Knitscene,* and *Love of Knitting.* She is the author of the popular Sock Yarn Shawls books, and you can also find dozens of her self-published patterns on Ravelry. In 2014, after a decade of testing municipal wastewater for a living, she retired her lab coat and safety glasses to work in her design business full-time. When she's not knitting, you can find Jen crocheting, reading, or trying new slow-cooker recipes she found online. She lives in Fox River Grove, Illinois, with her husband, Alex.

FIND JEN ONLINE!

See Jen's Designs at www.ravelry.com/designers/jen-lucas.
Check out Jen's website at www.jenlucasdesigns.com.
Follow Jen on Instagram @jenlucasdesigns.

What's your creative passion?
Find it at **ShopMartingale.com**
books • eBooks • ePatterns • blog • free projects
videos • tutorials • inspiration • giveaways

Martingale®
Create with Confidence